M000025123

Judaica

Written by Myra Yellin Outwater

Photography by Eric B. Outwater

4880 Lower Valley Road, Atglen, PA 19310 USA

Dedication

To a religion, which although often beleaguered, has inspired such creativity, originality, resourcefulness and love in its people.

To my Mother and Father, Sophie and Norman Yellin

To my aunt Lillian Altman

To my granddaughters Gabrielle, Caroline and Olivia Goldfarb who I expect will carry on the traditions.

And to my husband, Eric, who says that the best Jewish collectible of all is a Jewish wife.

Library of Congress Cataloging-in-Publication Data

Outwater, Myra Yellin.
    Judaica / written by Myra Yellin Outwater : photography by Eric B.Outwater.
        p.   cm.
    Includes bibliographical references and index.
    ISBN 0-7643-0785-1 (hc.)
    1. Judaism-- Liturgical objects. 2. Jewish art and symbolism.
I. Outwater, Eric Boe. II. Title.
NK1672.097   1999
296.4'6--dc21   98-55102
                                                      CIP

Copyright © 1999 by Myra Yellin Outwater

    All rights reserved. No part of this work may be reproduced or used in any form or by any means—graphic, electronic, or mechanical, including photocopying or information storage and retrieval systems—without written permission from the copyright holder.
    "Schiffer," "Schiffer Publishing Ltd. & Design," and the "Design of pen and inkwell" are registered trademarks of Schiffer Publishing Ltd.

Book Design by Anne Davidsen
Type set in Windsor BT/ Aldine 721 BT

ISBN: 0-7643-0785-1
Printed in China
1 2 3 4

Published by Schiffer Publishing Ltd.
4880 Lower Valley Road
Atglen, PA 19310
Phone: (610) 593-1777; Fax: (610) 593-2002
E-mail: Schifferbk@aol.com
Please visit our web site catalog at
www.schifferbooks.com

This book may be purchased from the publisher.
Include $3.95 for shipping.
Please try your bookstore first.
We are interested in hearing from authors
with book ideas on related subjects.
You may write for a free catalog.

In Europe, Schiffer books are distributed by
Bushwood Books
6 Marksbury Rd.
Kew Gardens
Surrey TW9 4JF England
Phone: 44 (0)181 392-8585; Fax: 44 (0)181 392-9876
E-mail: Bushwd@aol.com

Contents

Acknowledgements

Nancy Berman, director of the Skirball Cultural Center
and Museum
Muriel Berman, for her knowledge and enthusiasm
Brenda and Eva Bernstein
Elaine Silverman, manager of the gift shop at the National
Museum of American Jewish Histo. / in Philadelphia
Judy Murman of Congregation Keneseth Israel, Allen-
town, Pennsylvania
Ulysses Grant Dietz, curator of the Newark Museum
Judith Goldstein
Wilbur, Sara, and Paris Pierce
Peachy and Mark Levy and Dee and Arnold Kaplan who
shared their collections, knowledge, and enthusiasm
Eleanor Norwood and the Rabbi Abraham Feldman
Museum of Congregation Beth Israel
Lisa Fligelman of Audrey's at the Skirball Cultural Cen-
ter and Museum
Edythe Siegel
and Joe Langman, who kindled the flame

Introduction:
What is Judaica?

Twentieth century Judaica has become a wonderful mix of materials, artistic expressions and visual artistry. Silver Sabbath candle sticks, wooden matzah boxes, sculptural kiddush cups, illuminated framed mezuzahs, silver and bronze seder plates, and artistic tzedakah containers create Jewish pride and enhance the joy of the holidays. *in the spirit gallery*.

We have defined Judaica as all those objects used that enhance the celebration and adherence to Jewish rituals and mitzvot and reaffirm a Jewish identity and a connection to the history of the Jewish people.

Ever since the Diaspora, Judaism has become a home oriented religion and therefore has been an expanding need for home Judaica. And since most Jewish holidays center around home feasts and family dinners, Jews, whether rich or poor, have tried to enhance the beauty of their tables and the reverence of the day, by displaying ritual objects that not only aid in their observance but help beautify the home.

This book hopes to celebrate both the past and the present of the Jewish creative spirit by showing how the multi-culturalism of the Jewish experience has created Jewish objects designed to rekindle the Jewish religious spirit.

Art in Jewish Rituals

For centuries people have believed that there was a biblical injunction against Jewish art, and that Jewish artists were inhibited by the second commandment which admonished Jews, "Thou shalt not make unto thee a graven image even any manner of likeness of anything that is in heaven above or that is the earth beneath or that is in the water under the earth. Thou shalt not bow down to them or serve them." The fact that in biblical times Jewish artists avoided any figural references further confirmed this belief.

But in Exodus, the Lord issues specific details about how He wants the holy sanctuary for His laws to be built. His details include a gold, silver and brass ark for the Torah covered with blue, gold, purple and scarlet linens, topped with a crown of gold. Additional details specify that the ark be decorated with images of cherubim and flowers:

"And the cherubim shall spread out their wings on high, with their faces one to another....And thou shalt make a candlestick of pure gold and there shall be seven branches going out of the sides, three branches on one side and three branches on the other."

And the Lord further signals out a specific man, Bezalel, to carry out this work... "to devise skillful works, to work in gold, and in silver, and in brass, and in the cutting of stones for setting and carving of wood, to work in all manner of workmanship." Exodus. 31:1-8.

Later, in Exodus 37, Bezalel's craftsmanship, sense of design and artistry are detailed: his mastery as a goldsmith and his use of natural imagery. "How lovely are Thy tabernacles," says the psalmist. (Psalm 84).

Throughout the centuries, the rabbis decreed that Jews should glorify the Lord by creating beautiful objects in which to celebrate the Commandments and the Jewish holidays. And specifically the Talmudic rabbis exhorted the Jews to make beautiful sukkahs, beautiful lulav covers, beautiful shofars, beautiful fringes for tallit and beautiful scrolls for the Law bound in beautiful wrappings.

The result has been the creation of a particularly Jewish art with its own symbolism, iconography and calligraphy that include frequent illusions to Solomon's Temple in Jerusalem, the Star of David, the Lion of Judah and images of the Holy Land.

More than many other religions, Judaism has been a home-oriented religion in its observances and celebrations. And thus, individual Jews have tried to create personal sanctuaries to God, and while the text of the religion is read in the synagogues and temples, its heart and soul is nurtured by Jewish families in their homes.

The image of a portable ark is carved in the column of a second- or third-century synagogue in Capernaum, Israel. This is the earliest image of the Jewish people moving from place to place bringing with them an ark bearing the Torah. And through much of the twentieth century, the Jews continued to be a nomadic people traveling from country to country, carrying along with them only their Torah and their belief in one God.

But even while they have been a people of the Diaspora for more than 2000 years, a people in exile, the Jews have cherished a dream of one day returning to their spiritual homeland, the land of Israel.

And throughout all these wanderings, the Jewish people have steadfastly maintained their religious beliefs and adhered to their rituals by carrying along with them not only the teachings of the Torah, but religious articles to aid in their observances. And though they have wandered further and further away from the land of Israel, the physical orientation of their ark has continued to face towards the western wall in Jerusalem.

But paradoxically even as they maintained spiritual ties to the land of Israel, they adapted to their new homes and adopted many of the customs of the lands in which they lived. And beginning in the Middle Ages, there developed a new ritual art which reflected the lands they now called home.

Art historians can trace the countries of the Jewish Exodus. Jews expelled from Spain by the Spanish Inquisition in the 15th century carried with them Moorish designs and Spanish filigrees. Dutch and German Jews brought along pewter and baroque brass. Italian Jews brought with them objects showing an Italianate sweep and elegance. English Jews brought with them the classical stateliness of England. And soon these stylistic motifs combined to create new religious icons and objects. And it was not a surprise to see Spanish and Moroccan

Detail

One of the earliest carvings of a portable Torah ark. This ark of a temple set on wheels is carved on the capital of a column in a second or third century synagogue at Capernaum, Israel.

designs reappear in the homes and villages of Eastern Europe and Jewish religious items assume an internationalism reflecting centuries of imposed travel.

Today's Jewish ceremonial objects reflect the multiculturalism of these years of travel. And by examining each piece and its different stylistic motifs, designs and artistry, one can trace the migration of the Jews from Palestine to the lands of the Mediterranean, Spain, Eastern Europe, India, China and the United States and their return to Israel.

The late 19th and early twentieth century would result in one of the most important mass emigrations of the Jewish people. Eastern European immigrants would flee to America bringing with them, trunks full of clothes, a samovar, pots and pans, and often Sabbath candlesticks and a brass menorah for Hanukkah. In fact many of these immigrants would buy a new set of candlesticks or a new menorah before embarking on their new lives.

And it would be those years in eastern Europe that would have the most decisive impact on Jewish culture. And it would be those years in exile in Poland and in Russia that would nurture what would become a new Jewish artistic, literary and culinary rebirth. From those communities and shtetls would come many of the leaders of the American Jewish community and many of Israel's founding fathers.

The Statue of Liberty was a sign of freedom, opportunity and religious freedom for millions of immigrants. The words on its base were written by a Jewish poet Emma Lazarus, "Give me your tired, your poor, your huddled masses yearning to be free."

The Changing Forms and Shapes of Judaica

For years Jewish museums have spot-lighted those surviving antiques of the 16th, 17th, and 18th centuries as well as the sentimental remnants of the past brought to America by 19th and early twentieth century Jewish immigrants. And until the twentieth century many of these objects were venerated as much for sentimental as artistic value. But the birth of the state of Israel was not only a rebirth of the Jewish people, but a cause for reaffirmation of faith for many Jews who began search for Jewish objects to decorate their homes and to observe the holidays.

This book hopes to celebrate both the past and the present of the Jewish creative spirit by showing how the multi-culturalism of the twentieth century Jewish experience has created a new set of Jewish objects designed to rekindle the Jewish religious spirit.

When the Israelites of biblical times worshipped on the Temple Mount, they used as models for their religious objects, things in every day use. Since light has always played a significant role in religion, the candelabras for the Temple were traditional free standing, tree-branched candle holders. The first Hanukkah lamps were based on the traditional clay oil-lamps of the time and priestly robes, Torah covers, Torah crowns, and sanctuary arks were often indistinguishable from those used in other contemporary religious ceremonies of the day.

But once the Jewish people dispersed in the Diaspora, they began to adapt their customs and artifacts to those

Among the many treasured possessions that Jewish immigrants brought with them to America was the family's brass samovar. For many of these people gathering around a kitchen table for a cup of tea was part of the daily home life in the old country. *The National Museum of American Jewish History.*

of their new homes. And since Jews were not allowed to join guilds they had to depend on objects made by non-Jewish artists for their ritual use.

The wealthy Jews of the day had the means to buy special objects intended only for religious practice. They would commission silver goblets for kiddush, silver plates for the seder, candelabra for Shabbat, and through use and often the addition of a Hebrew engraving, sanctify them into Jewish ceremonial objects. Wine goblets intended for church worship became kiddush cups, Elijah's cups, Havdalah and marriage cups. Silver boxes became estrog containers. Snuff boxes became Havdalah spice boxes. And later in the 18th and 19th centuries, oyster plates became prototypes for Seder plates and beer steins became hand washers. Artisans and scribes inscribed Hebrew prayers onto these silver, gold, copper, or brass items transforming them into future cherished family heirlooms. In fact today, many traditional Shabbat candlesticks are only known to be "Jewish" through use. But poorer Jews had to rely more on their ingenuity than their pocket books. Many would use objects in daily use for religious purposes. Every day candle holders would also become Sabbath lights. Ordinary goblets would have dual roles for the Kiddush. Other more inventive Jews would improvise and create their own religious objects such as this hand-made hand-washer or this former beer stein, now a hand washer (see page 11).

Traditional 19th century-early 20th century candlesticks used for Shabbat. Silver and brass. Warsaw. 1900. Since Jews were often among the poorer members of society, until the late 19th century most of them sought out cheaper materials such as pewter and brass for their ritual objects. Later it became more common to use brass and silver. Until the nineteenth century, European Jews lived under many economic sanctions and because they were not allowed to join guilds, there were no Jewish artisans. Therefore since Jews had to buy their ceremonial objects from non-Jewish artisans, it was common for Jews to convert secular objects into religious uses. *Estate of Mrs. Mayer Yellin and Mrs. Sophie Yellin.* $500.

Boris Schatz, Ludwig Wolpert, and the Bezalel School

In 1906 a Lithuanian-born Jew named Boris Schatz had a dream. An ardent Zionist, he decided to found an arts and crafts school in Israel. Naming it "the Bezalel School" after the first artist mentioned in the Bible in the book of Exodus, his goal was to produce hand-made secular and Jewish ritual items that looked Jewish and reflected the culture of the Jewish people. Schatz hoped that the sales of these works to the increasing number of pilgrims and tourists visiting the Holy Land would support his Jewish arts and crafts movement. Incorporating the indigenous styles of Jerusalem artisans- Yemenite silversmiths, Moroccan brass and copper workers, Arabic carpet weavers, Syrian metal inlay designers, as well as wood and ivory carvers, Schatz also tried to create a uniquely Eretz- Israel style of folk art. Heavily influenced by the Arts and Crafts movement of America and the Zionist dreams of Herzl, Schatz incorporated the Hebrew language in his designs.

But it wouldn't be until 1926 with the arrival of a German metalsmith, Ludwig Wolpert (1900-1982), that Schatz would realize his dream of creating a Jewish style. Wolpert not only incorporated Jewish images into his work, but created a stylized calligraphic Hebrew lettering.

Although Schatz was forced to close the school for lack of funds in 1929, by 1935 a new Bezalel School opened with new faces and a new artistic philosophy. From then on the Bezalel artists would forgo the old world romanticism of Schatz, who had died still fund raising for his school in 1932, and create what would become modern Judaica and elevate the ritual object into museum quality.

Many credit Wolpert, who had studied at the Frankfort School of Arts and Crafts before emigrating to Palestine in 1929, with pioneering and founding modern Judaica.

And after years at the Bezalel School, in 1956 he was asked to come to the Jewish Museum in New York and become the artist in residence at the Tobe Pascher workshop, and train a new generation of artists in Judaica. Wolpert, who had been exposed to the Bauhaus movement in Germany, brought with him not only the spirit of the Bezalel School, but the stylistic modernism of Europe. He became one of the first to create a series of religious objects that were both artistic and functional. It was Wolpert who was one of the first modern artists to engrave a cursive, decorative Hebrew calligraphy on silver goblets, plates, menorahs and boxes.

One of Wolpert's most famous students would be the Israeli artist Moshe Zabari. Later, Zabari succeeded Wolpert and became head of the Tobe Pascher School until 1988 when he returned to Israel. Zabari's works are among the most coveted by collectors of modern Judaica.

Shabbat candlesticks. Hammered silver. 1950s. Ludwig Yehuda Wolpert. Wolpert is credited with modernizing the lines and designs of twentieth century Judaica. These candlesticks are among his best work. *Rabbi Abraham Feldman Museum of the Congregation Beth Israel.* $2000.

Twentieth Century Judaica

The Old Testament has always been a source of inspiration for artists of all religions. Michelangelo is still most remembered for his sculptures of David and Moses. Rembrandt and Jacob van Ruysdael were just two who frequently painted Jewish models and Jewish synagogues. In the late 19th and early twentieth centuries Jewish artists such as Chagall and Soutine would turn to their Jewish roots for their artistic inspiration. Twentieth century Americans such as Leonard Baskin and Ben Shahn created their versions of the Haggadah.

The late Hana Geber (1910-1990) is one of the many twentieth century artists who created Judaica that was an artistic as well as a religious and emotional statement about her experiences fleeing the Holocaust. Agam is another colorful twentieth century Israeli artist who makes unusual Judaica.

The 1960s and 1970s were a period during which many Americans turned away from the traditional idea of America as a melting pot and craved more ethnic identity. Blacks wanted Black Studies. East Asian studies sprung up on American university campuses. The Women's movement began to fight for more gender studies. People began to wear the colors of their national origins on their tee-shirts and their cars and the Jews, too, began to turn inward and reassess their religious separateness and formed Jewish Day Schools outside what were traditional Jewish communities.

Jewish artists have always looked to the stories of the Bible to find symbols to represent the holidays. But today these stories are imbued with a new aesthetic that has resulted in not only a mix of high art, but an engaging whimsical folk art that celebrates both the Israel of the past, the Israel of the Bible and the Israel of the present.

Not only have these objects sparked a renaissance in the observance of Jewish rituals, but a love of the rituals of the religion and the establishment of a new twentieth-century Jewish spirit.

Today Judaica is proudly displayed in Reform as well as Orthodox and Conservative Jewish homes. And not only do twentieth century Jews cherish the old brass menorahs, candlesticks and silver kiddush cups that were handed down from their grandparents, but they collect and admire Judaica objects made from silver, ceramic, stone, glass, stainless steel, aluminum and carved wood.

Collecting Judaica

The birth of Israel in 1948 created greater demands for collectible Judaica. And almost immediately after the establishment of the Jewish state, there was a mass production of touristic objects. Carvers had been producing olivewood souvenirs for tourists to the Holy Land since the 19th century, but after the birth of Israel, it became an industry. Soon there were olivewood camels, olivewood book covers, olivewood estrog and olivewood boxes everywhere.

Another new growth industry was that of the green patinaed copper wares. Soon factories were producing green plates, candlesticks, menorahs, estrog boxes, and various souvenirs. One of the best known of these factories was the Pal Bel factory. Soon there was a surfeit of this new style Judaica and Jews who had long been ashamed or afraid to express their Judaism openly became eager consumers, displayed this new Judaica everywhere.

Today, Judaica can be classified as pre-1948 Israel, post-1948 Israel and post-Six Day War. Pre-Israel objects were mostly made from pewter, silver and brass. Post-Israel Judaica would be olivewood and green metal. But after that one week in June, 1967, and that swift war that resulted in a spirited and dramatic recovery of Jewish religious sites: the Western Wall, Hebron and the caves of the Patriarchs, the West Bank, Bethlehem, Jericho, and the Sinai peninsula as well as the reunification of Jerusalem, there was a new Jewish spirit. That victory would instill in American Jewry a new pride and desire to assert their Jewishness. As more Jews chose to openly display their Judaism, Jewish artists responded boldly and imaginatively to the challenge to create new Jewish ceremonial items.

What is most extraordinary about this explosion of post-Six Day War Judaica is the thoughtfulness of these Jewish artisans. Looking back at the old traditional pieces, one senses a lack of passion in the way the majority of these objects were fashioned, adorned and constructed. Most of the objects— the goblets, spice boxes, and candlesticks— look like secular objects transformed. What is most exciting about the new Judaica is the way individual artists express their passion about the religion by creating objects that not only celebrate the rituals but celebrate the spirit of the holidays.

There are many kinds of Judaica collections and as many different kinds of collectors. There are collectors who only collect objects of artistic value and there are collectors who only collect historically relevant objects. There are collectors who only collect rare ceremonial and ritual items. There are collectors who specialize only in American Judaica. There are those who only collect ritual items and those who specialize in secular Judaica preferring to make more of a historical statement than one governed by aesthetics. There are also those Jews who collect anything Jewish.

Serious collectors of Judaica frequent Sotheby's and Christie's auctions and buy rare pieces for upwards of hundreds of thousands of dollars. Other equally dedicated but not as deep-pocketed collectors frequent the auctions and the dealers, but also spend endless hours pouring through antiques shops and ephemera sales to assemble their collections.

And finally there are the collectors, who proud of their Jewishness, collect only with their heart. It is to these collectors that we dedicate this book and hope that we have assembled a popular assortment of Judaica showing both historical trends in the designs of Jewish ceremonial objects from the late 18th century through the present as well as some of the best of twentieth-century Judaica.

This book is intended to give an overview of the field. Our list of contemporary artists is not intended to be definitive, but just an attempt to spotlight a few of the very gifted and talented artists who are creating the Judaica of the twentieth century.

Since the birth of Israel, modern Jewish artists have created new Jewish ritual objects as well as encouraged new Jewish customs. Left to right. A marriage box to save the pieces of the shattered glass of the marriage goblet, a hand-painted wedding plate, a Ketubah case to display the marriage contract, the Ketubah, a hanging Sabbath candle lamp and a hand-painted marriage goblet. Today artists create many new individual ceremonial objects so that every member of the family can participate in all the rituals.
Marriage box. S. Kagan. $395.
Wedding plate. Hand-painted porcelain. S. Kagan/I. Puski. $325.
Ketubah box. S. Kagan/I. Puski. *in the spirit gallery.* $2400.
Candlesticks. brass. S. Kagan. $1500.
Wedding cup. Hand-painted porcelain. S. Kagan/I. Puski. *in the spirit gallery.* $185.

Pricing Judaica

It is more difficult to price Judaica than most other fields since the market place is narrow and exclusive. Wealthy Jews have been collecting top of the line Judaica for hundreds of years. Many treasured heirlooms have been passed down in families and have never been priced in the market place. In addition, many older pieces have retained their religious functions and as such it seems irreverent to assign a monetary value to them.

Another problem is that the field of American Judaica is relatively new and uncharted. Most dealers do not deal exclusively with a Jewish market, and collectors must forage to find exclusively Jewish items, and either make their own market or compete with generic prices.

In our pricing we have depended on dealers, checked the market place and made some calculated assumptions.

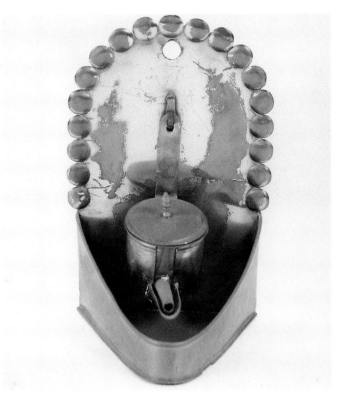

Washing cup. Copper hand-chased. Circa 1600s. Although the wealthier Jews were able to buy special items for their worship and celebration of the Jewish holidays, the poorer Jews had to be more creative and improvise. This copper mug was originally a beer stein. With the addition of a Hebrew blessing it becomes a hand washing basin to be used to wash the hands as proscribed in the Passover seder. *Estate of Gloria Abrams.* $1800.

"Al Nitilat Yadayim."....for the washing of the hands. Folk art piece by J. Stuart Green circa 1940. Before the birth of the state of Israel, there were few places where Jews could buy ceremonial items such as hand washing basins. Therefore many made their own such as this example of Jewish ingenuity. *Brenda Bernstein collection.*

Thus we have only priced objects where it seems appropriate as well as possible. And in cases where an object is a one of a kind and purchased more than ten years ago, we have not even tried to assign a present day value.

In pricing modern Judaica by contemporary artists we have judged their quality and the marketplace in placing our values, assuming that these pieces will retain and increase their value in the future.

In conclusion, we add another caveat. Value is determined only in the market place. And when collecting it is important to balance desire with economic reality. 'Is it worth it?' is a question often asked and the answer is a difficult one.

As in many one of a kind items, a collector must decide if an item meets personal collecting needs. We are reminded of one collector whose keen eye ferreted out a historic document worth thousands out of a pile of yellowed papers all selling for under $100. And then just a few days later, over-paid for another object just because it piqued his fancy. Years later looking over his collection, the resulting spectacular assemblage was a result of both good and wise choices as well as a few flighty indulgences.

Twentieth-century Judaica has become a wonderful mix of materials, artistic expressions, and visual artistry. Silver Sabbath candle sticks, painted wooden matzah boxes, sculptural kiddush cups, illuminated framed mezuzahs, silver and bronze seder plates, and artistic tzedakah containers create Jewish pride and enhance the joy of the holidays.

It is also important to remember that a good Judaica collection will probably be a series of hits and misses, objects of both excellent quality, artistry and craftsmanship and also pieces of good hearted schmaltz. Collections can concentrate on objects, historical documents and ephemera, or just objects of social commentary about the Jewish condition. Collections also usually include one or two objects of just sentimental and nostalgic value. Who doesn't remember the unobtrusive presence of the lowly Blue Box, the loud grating noises of a metal grogger, the wine stained pages of the Maxwell House Hagaddah or the presence on a holiday table of a bottle of seltzer with its stainless steel spritzer?

In this book we have chosen to create a visual history of the religious life of the Jewish people by showing objects that celebrate the Jewish spirit, the Jewish intellect and the religious passion that have kept the Jewish people intact for so many generations.

L'Chaim! To life!

During the late 1890s a young Zionist artist named Boris Schatz founded an arts and craft school in Jerusalem. Named after the earliest known Jewish artist Bezalel the school produced a large body of work including this brass Passover plate. *Rabbi Abraham Feldman Museum of the Congregation Beth Israel.* $1600.

A detail from the plate. The nine vignettes around the rim of the plate illustrate the story of the Passover song "Chad Gad Ya- one little goat." "One little goat I bought for two zuzim."

Havdalah plate. Silver. Ludwig Yehuda Wolpert. 1950s. Wolpert is considered the father of modern Judaica. A Frankfurt trained silversmith, Wolpert worked at the Bezalel School in Israel until 1956 when he was hired by the Jewish Museum in New York to establish its own school of Jewish art. Wolpert's trademark was his use of Hebrew calligraphy on silver. *Rabbi Abraham Feldman Museum of the Congregation Beth Israel.*

Havdalah set. Silver. Ludwig Yehuda Wolpert. 1950s. Another example of Wolpert's artistry. *Rabbi Abraham Feldman Museum of the Congregation Beth Israel.* $1000.

Fish plate. "I ate I blessed and I was satisfied..grace after the meal. Hand painted porcelain. S. Kagan/I. Puski. Judaica can be objects used specifically for ceremonial and ritual use as well as objects in everyday use. We classify Judaica as any object which helps affirm Jewish identity. *in the spirit gallery.* $250.

Bagel-shaped container. China. Years ago bagels were a necessity for any Jewish breakfast or brunch or dairy meal. Today bagels have become an international snack food and are found all over the world -in delis as well as fast food restaurants. Bagels have even gone designer and it is no longer a surprise to find a bagel flecked with sundried tomatoes or olives as well as the more traditional poppy and sesame seeds. *Congregation Keneseth Israel.* $25.

13

Sampler. 1900. American. While many Jews quickly assimilated into American society, many struggled with the question of how to maintain their Jewish identities in this new land. *Private collection.*

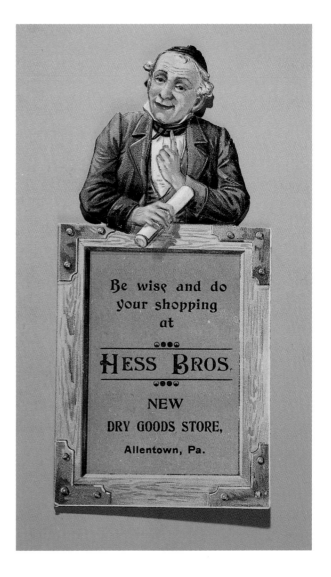

Trade card. 1900s. America. Hess Brothers remained a well known department store in Allentown, Pennsylvania through the 1980s. Like many Jewish shop keepers, the Hess Brothers were proud of their Jewish identity. Placing a man with a skullcap on an advertising card was a deliberate statement. It also capitalized on the popular notion that Jews were smart businessmen and offered good values. *Private collection.* $100.

Chapter 1. The Sabbath

Shabbat candlesticks, kiddush cups, challah plates, challah covers, challah knives.

"And the heaven and the earth were finished, and all the host of them. And on the seventh day God finished His work which He had made; and He rested on the seventh day from all His work which he had made. And God blessed the seventh day, and hallowed it, because that in it He rested from all His work which God in creating had made." Genesis 2:1-3.

And thus was born the concept of the Sabbath, *Shabbat.*

Perhaps the most popular image of a Shabbat observance for many Americans, Jews and non-Jews, occurs in the Broadway musical "Fiddler on the Roof." The mother puts a shawl over her head, lights the Sabbath candles and recites the Shabbat prayer.

"Baruch Atah Adonai Eloheynu Melech ha olum asher kid'shahnu B'mitz vo tav v'tzi vanu l'had lik ner shel Shabbat."

"Blessed art Thou, O Lord, our God, king of the universe, who has commanded us to light the Sabbath lights."

Then as the candles flicker and glow, the father raises his kiddush cup and recites the Kiddush, the prayer over the wine.

"Baruch Atah Adonai Eloheynu Melech ha olum boray p'ree hagafen,"

"Blessed be Thou, O Lord, our God, king of the Universe, who gives us fruit of the vine,"

and then he raises the braided bread,

"Baruch Atah Adonai Eloheynu Melech ha olum hamotzi lechem min ha oretz."

"Blessed art Thou, O Lord, our God, king of the universe who has given us bread from the earth."

Of all the Jewish holidays the most sacred is the Sabbath, the seventh day of the Jewish week. Each Friday afternoon, Orthodox Jews begin to prepare for the Sabbath, or Shabbat, which begins at sundown. But while the men in the family leave work early and prepare to go to services, it is the women who prepare the home for Shabbat and make it a religious sanctuary for Shabbat worship. A holiday table is set. A special meal is made and the evening is greeted as if it were a special guest, hence the term the Sabbath Queen.

Shabbat, Passover, Shavuot and Succoth are the only holidays and feast days mentioned in the Torah. But only the Shabbat is mentioned in the Ten Commandments.

The Star of David has been a symbol of Judaism since the second century B.C.E. This is a carving found on a second or third century synagogue in Capernaum, Israel.

Many think that breadfruit is the manna of the Exodus.

15

The fourth commandment reads, "Remember the Sabbath and keep it holy. Six days shalt thou labor, and do thy work. But the seventh day is the Sabbath of the Lord thy God: in it thou shalt not do any work, thou, nor thy son nor thy daughter, thy manservant, nor thy maidservant, nor thy cattle, nor thy stranger that is within thy gates."

For the Orthodox this is interpreted that they will not do any secular work of any kind, but they will spend the day contemplating the grace and goodness of God. Even the Lord, says the Bible, rested from his labors on the seventh day after creating the world in six days. And in strictest tradition, the Talmud lists specific forbidden labors.

The earliest mention of Shabbat was in Exodus when the Lord commanded the Israelites in the desert to gather a double portion of manna on the sixth day making the seventh day, the Sabbath, a day of rest. Later it was the Pharisees who first established the ritual of the lighting of the Sabbath candles.

The Sabbath meal is the highlight of the week for the Jewish family. A white starched table cloth is laid on the table. A special meal is prepared and the mother of the family lights the Sabbath lights and slices the Challah bread. The father says a blessing over the wine and the entire family gives tzedakah in thanksgiving for the blessings that God has provided.

Today the candles are lit at sunset and in many metropolitan areas the exact times are listed each week in the Friday newspaper.

For many Jews the observation of the Sabbath is home oriented and limited to four rituals- the lighting of the Sabbath candles, the blessing of the wine, the blessing of the challah bread and then the next night, a celebration of the conclusion of the Sabbath with the Havdalah service at sundown Saturday evening.

There must always be at least two candles lit during the Sabbath to symbolize "light" and "darkness" and correspond to the biblical dictum to "observe and remember" the Sabbath. In some families many candles are lit in order to involve other members of the family in the holiday observance.

The braided egg bread, the challah, while in its present form, is of eastern European and German origin, also has biblical significance. In the Bible the Hebrew translation for challah refers to the portion of dough removed from each baking of bread and given to the priest in ancient Israel. Later it became the portion burned after the destruction of the Temple.

Usually two loaves are placed on the Sabbath table to remind the Jews of the double portion of manna sent down from Heaven to the Israelites in the desert during the Exodus.

The Sabbath is the only Jewish holiday where the woman conducts most of the home rituals and is responsible for setting the proper stage for its observance. And for many, the real Sabbath Queen is the woman of the house. This is her holiday, and as she cleans the house, sets the table, prepares the meal, it is she who becomes a Sabbath Queen.

The Sabbath table is set with a challah that is covered with a richly decorated cloth and placed on a special Sabbath plate or board. Usually there is a special knife to cut the bread, a special silver wine cup for the Kiddush, the blessing of the wine, and a holiday table cloth. The candles are either lit at sundown or when the family gathers for dinner.

When it comes to Jewish ceremonial objects, the most commonly found in Jewish families is a cherished set of Sabbath candlesticks, a silver Kiddush cup and a Challah plate. Many families treasure the brass candlesticks brought over from Europe by their grandparents. Today Jews buy candlesticks made by contemporary silversmiths, pewtersmiths, glass blowers and potters.

With the birth of Israel, Israeli artisans created a new kind of Judaica, copper and green trimmed ritual objects, and soon tourists were buying the green and copper candlesticks and challah plates. Sabbath cloths and challah covers began to show Arabic influences.

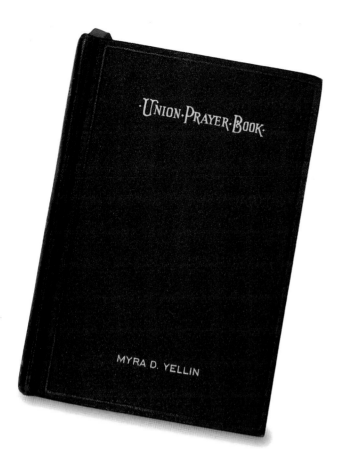

Sabbath (Shabbat)

Shabbos, Shabbat, or the Hebrew Sabbath begins Friday evening at sundown. The woman of the house says a blessing over the Sabbath lights and the challah, a braided egg bread. In Hebrew the challah was the portion of dough removed from each baking and given to the priest in ancient Israel, or the portion burned after the destruction of the Temple. Next the father says the Kiddush, the blessing over the wine. Kiddush comes from the Hebrew word "Kodesh" meaning holy. A Sabbath table is set with at least two candlesticks, a Kiddush cup, a challah board or dish, a challah knife, and a challah cover.

American Jewry is divided into three branches- Orthodox, Conservative and Reform. Each group has its own prayer book, customs and Sabbath service. This is the Union Prayer book written by rabbis of the Reform movement. It is customary for congregations to give Jewish children bibles, prayer books or kiddush cups on the occasion of their bar or bat mitzvahs and confirmations.

A sterling silver kiddush sculpture of a wine goblet with cups. Hungarian. *in the spirit gallery.* $1200.

Kiddush cups. Silver. Every Jewish home has at least one silver kiddush cup. *The National Museum of American Jewish History.* $100-250.

17

Kiddush Goblet/Shabbat candlesticks. Ceramic. Garson/Pakele. USA. Contemporary ceramic Shabbat candlesticks and kiddush cup made by Colorado artists Susan Garson and Tom Pakele who create contemporary whimsical ritual objects, filled with symbolism reminiscent of Marc Chagall and other naive artists. *in the spirit gallery.* $225/185.

Popular folk figures. 1900s. Composition. Syrocco (from Syracuse). These two figures of "bubbe" and "zaydie" were originally made in Lithuania, but the family of artists moved to Syracuse, New York. These sentimental depictions of the old world "bubbe" carrying her prayer book with a Jewish star and the "zaydie" carrying his tallis and tefillin were popular among Jews in the first part of the twentieth century. They were sold at the 1939 World's Fair. The collector says that her grandmother had a set in her home when she was growing up. *Private collection.*

Sabbath lamp. Alabaster. Yemenite. 1920s-1940s. Most Sabbath lamps, Judenstern, are in the shape of a Jewish star and are made out of brass. *Private collection.*

Sabbath (S.Kagan) Detail.

Candlesticks. Silver. Warsaw silver. *Estate of Sophie Yellin*. $1900.

Sabbath candlesticks. Brass. Eastern European circa 1900s. Shabbat candlesticks can be ornate or simple brass candle holders like these. This set was probably brought over from Poland in the late 1890s. *Estate of Jennie Fish*. $100.

19

Candlesticks. Brass. Late 1890s. *Estate of Sophie Yellin*. $90.

Sabbath candlesticks. Hammered Silver. Ludwig Wolpert.
Rabbi Abraham Feldman Museum of the Congregation Beth Israel.
$2000.

Candlesticks. Sterling/brass. Hana Geber. *in the spirit gallery*. $2400.

Candle holder for Shabbat. Metal/glass. 1960s. Israel. Post-Israeli
Independence Judaica was often made of this kind of green patina
metal. One of the best known manufacturers was Pal-Bel. This well
worn Shabbat set was bought in Israel in the 1960s. *Collection of
Mrs. Louis Altman.* $100.

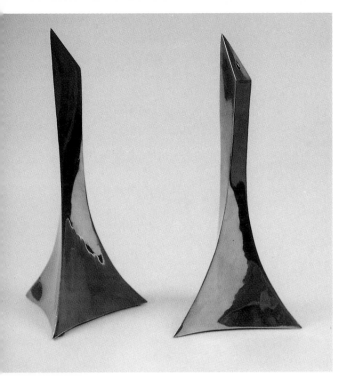

Candlesticks. Cast aluminum. S. Kagan. These sleek modern candlesticks are a far cry from the more ornate traditional ones used in 19th century Europe. *in the spirit gallery.* $1800.

The field of Judaica has attracted many outstanding artists in the twentieth century. The work of Hana Geber is immediately recognizable. Twisted forms and shapes writhe in horror reminding the viewer of the destruction of the millions of Jews in Europe during the Holocaust. Geber was born in Prague in 1910. Like many of the cultured and wealthy Jews of the time, her family was irreligious. And it would not be until adulthood, that Geber, the daughter of an ardent Zionist would identify with the religious side of her nature. Geber's religious odyssey began in 1939 when, hoping to escape Hitler, she tried to flee Prague. While on the train she was approached by a Nazi officer. Later she recalled that incident. "Something gave me courage: I asked to speak to him privately and looked him straight in the eye and said, `I am Jewish. The man in the corner is my husband and he is Jewish. We are fleeing from your Fuhrer.' I told him that he could save his soul by saving ours."

A modern platter to hold the Sabbath candlesticks. "Remember the Sabbath Day and Keep it Holy" is inscribed in both English and Hebrew. Often Jewish ceremonial objects have both English and Hebrew inscriptions. *National Museum of American Jewish History.*

Shabbat candlestick. 24 caret gold over bronze. B. Shohan. Israeli. The two top right points of this "Shin" candle holder holds the two Sabbath candles. The symbol "shin" refers to "Shaddai," a name reserved for God. *in the spirit gallery.* $395.

Candlesticks "Family of Man." Cast aluminum. S. Kagan. Judaism has always been a family oriented religion and the celebration of the Sabbath is one of the most family oriented rituals. While the Torah says that two candles must be lit on the Sabbath to recall the double portion of manna given to the Israelites while they were in wilderness, in recent years there has been more latitude in this Sabbath adherence. Some families will light a candle for each member of the family during Sabbath. *in the spirit gallery*. $595.

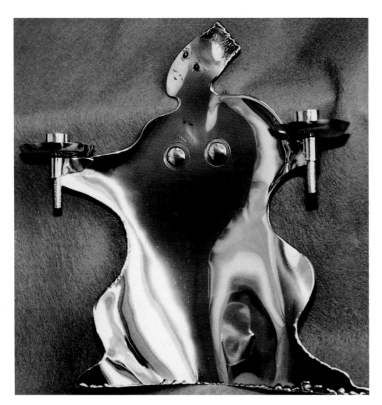

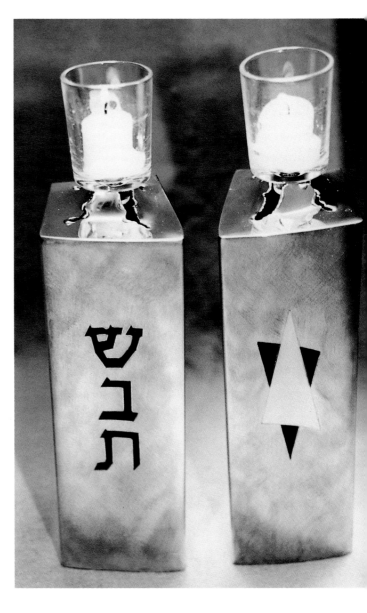

Above: Sabbath candle holders. Pewter with sterling silver candle cylinders. "The Sabbath Queen." 1994. Judith E. Goldstein. USA. The symbol is obvious, the universal female form, the Sabbath queen and the woman-wife-mother who holds the Sabbath together. Her hair is arranged like a crown. The Hebrew letters for Shabbat are patinated on the back in black. *Photography by Judith E. Goldstein*. $600.

Right: Sabbath candle holders. Pewter. "Sabbath Shapes and Reflections." 1996. Judith E. Goldstein. USA.
"The collapsed flowing body shapes remind us that our world has varying and fleeting realities. The only reminder of eternity and the presence of God is the star of David and the Hebrew letters for Shabbat." *Photography by Judith E. Goldstein*. $950.

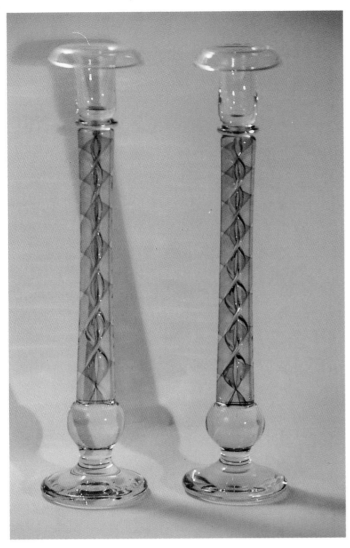

Sabbath glass candlesticks. *The National Museum of American Jewish History*. $300.

Shabbat candle holder. Piper- Strong. This colorful cast-iron holder evokes the mystical fervor and enthusiasm of the Hasidism. A bride and groom whirl around the wedding chuppah crowned by the Sabbath lights. *The National Museum of American Jewish History*. $100.

Sabbath candle holders. Johanna Bloch. USA. This clay Sabbath candle holder was made by Johanna Bloch as a class project. The California teenager wanted to create her own Sabbath gift for her parents.

Candlesticks. Wood. Traditionally Eastern European women would cover their face when they said the blessings over the Sabbath lights. Notice the image inside the center of the Star of David of a woman covering her face. *The National Museum of American Jewish History*. $150.

23

Shabbat candlesticks. Ceramic. B. Lenore. USA. This design, while whimsical and light hearted, also makes architectural references to the Temple in Jerusalem. *in the spirit gallery.* $295.

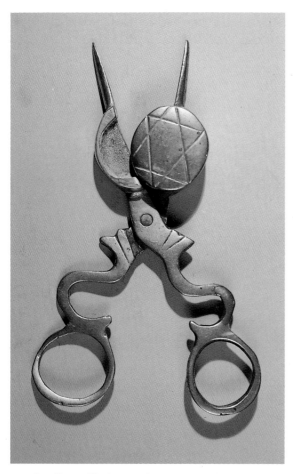

Candle snuffer. Brass. circa 1870s. This instrument was used to snuff the Sabbath candles. Notice the Star of David motif.

Candlesticks. Aluminum. Brenda Zaltas. Since the destruction of the Great Temple in Jerusalem in the Hanukkah story, artists have made references to its architecture. These ultra modern candle sticks show a strong geometric design, but they also make references to columns, pillars and steps of the ancient Temple in Jerusalem. *in the spirit gallery.* $295.

Candlesticks. Ceramic. Garson/Pakele. USA. These whimsical candlesticks use African and biblical imagery. Like the animals in Noah's ark, these also go two by two. *National Museum of American Jewish History*. $220 each.

Silver kiddush cups. These three traditional kiddush cups show signs of wear, tear and tarnish. Cups like these, decorated with Hebrew engravings, the Star of David, and natural images can be found in almost every Jewish home. *Congregation Keneseth Israel*. $50-200.

Kiddush cup. Silver. 1960s. This was given as a baby gift. It is traditional to give Jewish babies gifts of religious significance. *Laurence Goldfarb Collection*. $100.

The Sabbath. S. Kagan. Detail.

Kiddush cup. Silver. Mexico. 1970s. Notice that the designs show Mexican natural imagery. *Laurence Goldfarb Collection.* $200.

Kiddush cup. Silver. circa 1800s. This cup belonged to Rebecca Gratz, one of the best known Jewish women living in colonial Philadelphia. The cup was given by Gratz to the Mikveh Israel synagogue, the oldest synagogue in Philadelphia. It is signed R.G. on the bottom. Mikveh Israel is now housed on Independence Square in *The National Museum of American Jewish History.* *Private collection.*

Kiddush goblet. Silver. Circa 1850s. This goblet was presented to Herman Gratz, another member of the Gratz family on the occasion of his 70th birthday. *Private collection.*

Kiddush goblet. Silver. Revolutionary War era. Presented to the right honorable Benjamin Nones who served with the rank of Major in the Revolutionary War. Nones, who was in business with Haym Solomon, was elected president of Mikveh Israel in 1771 and wrote an impassioned essay in defense of Judaism. This cup was made by Joseph Shoemaker, a Philadelphia silversmith. (1793-1839.) "Humbly presented to the right honorable Benjamin Nones for his dedicated service to the Jewish Community of Philadelphia." *Private collection.*

Kiddush cup. Silver. *The National Museum of American Jewish History.* $150.

Kiddush goblet. Silver/bronze. Hana Geber. *in the spirit gallery.* $975.

Kiddush Goblet. Silver repousse. 1869. Given to Mr. Strauss who was a shohet, a kosher butcher on June 2, 1869. At his death it was given to Rabbi Feldman who gave it to the temple in 1972. *Rabbi Abraham Feldman Museum of the Congregation Beth Israel.*

Kiddush goblets. Hana Geber. *Nancy Berman and Alan Bloch Collection.*

Kiddush cups. Silver. R. Landau. Israel. *in the spirit gallery*. $975.

Kiddush cup. Moshe Zabari. Israeli. Zabari is considered by many the most important Judaica artist of the twentieth century. A student of Wolpert, he moved to New York and headed the Tobe Pascher school at the Jewish Museum in New Year, until he returned to Jerusalem in 1988. Within recent years he has created a series of works that make statements about Jewish history and Jewish philosophy. His works incorporate both a strong sense of the Jewish religion and a strong artistic sense. *Audrey's, the shop at the Skirball Cultural Center and Museum.* $4100.

Zig-zag Kiddush goblet. Silver. *in the spirit gallery*. $185.

Kiddush Goblet. Silver. Hana Geber. This was a personal gift from the artist. *Nancy Berman Collection*.

Kiddush cup. Pewter. "Stephanie's Dove." 1992.
Judith E. Goldstein. USA. This Bat Mitzvah Kiddush cup was a
gift to the artist's daughter, Stephanie and symbolizes her
gentleness, (the dove) her commitment to her Judaism (star of
David) and all her promise (the rays of light.) *Photography by
Judith E. Goldstein.* $800.

Kiddush cup. Pewter and ebony. "Star of David" Kiddush Cup.
Judith E. Goldstein. 1989. This cup symbolizes the strength of
King David's faith. Collection of Allen M. Goldstein. *Photography
by Judith E. Goldstein.* $700.

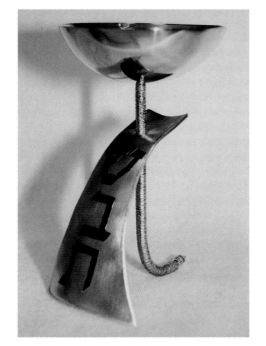

Kiddush cup. Pewter. "Sabbath Balance." 1994. Judith E.
Goldstein. USA. The Sabbath is a time to regain the emotional
balance of the week. The two bases symbolize the duality of the
Sabbath observance, the two candles, the two challahs, and now two
bases to choose from which to hold the kiddush cup. *Photography by
Judith E. Goldstein.* $300.

Kiddush cup. Silver/titanium. Ari Ofrir. Israel.
Audrey's at the Skirball Cultural Center and Museum. $550.

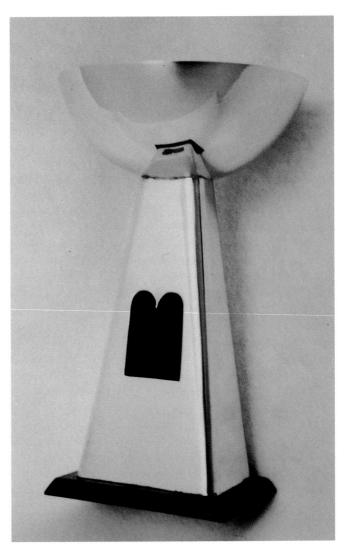

Kiddush cup. Pewter/ebony wood. "Offering" The Ten Commandments Kiddush cup. 1991. *Judith E. Goldstein. Photography by Judith E. Goldstein.* $700.

Kiddush cup. Silver. Titanium. Ari Ofrir. Israel. *Audrey's at the Skirball Cultural Center and Museum.* $550.

Kiddush goblet and Shabbat candlestick. Ceramic. Sharon Garson and Tom Pakele. This whimsical kiddush cup and Sabbath candlestick combines imagery from the Bible, nature and the shtetels of eastern Europe. *The National Museum of American Jewish History.* $220.

Glass goblet. Engraved. Steve Resnick. USA. 195. Resnick has created a series of engraved glass goblets for ceremonial use. The white one is engraved with the kiddush, the blue is designed as a Bar Mitzvah goblet and the pink one is a Miriam's goblet, a new design to enable women to participate in the Passover seder. *The National Museum of American Jewish History.* $275.

Above: Kiddush goblets. Glass. Kerry Feldman. Colorado. These goblets are engraved with the Hebrew prayers. A Star of David is engraved on its base.

Right: Kiddush goblet. Pewter/glass. The Liberty Goblet. Frequently artists express their nationality through their designs. Judaism has flourished in the United States. Since the end of the 19th century, America has become the promised land of opportunity and freedom for millions of East European Jews. *The National Museum of American Jewish History.* $60.

31

Kiddush cups. Silver. Stemmed goblet kiddush cups with the
traditional decorations- Hebrew letters and a stylized bunch of
grapes. The symbol of a bunch of grapes refers to the messengers
who were sent ahead when the Israelites were in the wilderness and
returned with grapes showing that there was fertile land ahead of
them. It is now one of the symbols of the Israeli nation. *Laurence,
Andrew, and Alexander Goldfarb Collection.* $100 each.

Kiddush goblet. Glass. Kerry
Feldman. USA.

Kiddush goblet. Glass. Kerry
Feldman. USA.

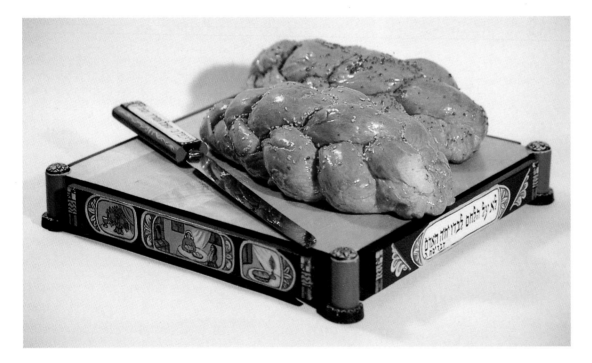

Above: Challah board and Challah knife. Hand-painted wood. S.
Kagan/I. Puski. The sides of this challah board shows scenes from
Sabbath observations. On one side is written the Hamotzi, the
blessing over the bread. "Blessed art thou O Lord our God who has
commanded us this day to eat bread from the earth." On the other
side is written. "Not by bread alone doth man live." *in the spirit
gallery.* board $500, knife $150.

Right: Sabbath. S. Kagan(detail)

Challah board. Engraved glass. Steve Resnick. USA. Crystal engraved Challah board and Challah knife with an olive branch design. Steve Resnick. "Hamotzi" means bread. *The Museum of American Jewish History*. board $200, knife $150.

Sabbath knife. 19th century. Probably German. This unique pocket knife reads Holy Sabbath. It not only has a knife but a corkscrew for the wine. 18th and 19th century Jews believed that it was unlucky to place a bare-bladed knife on the Sabbath table. *Private collection*.

Sabbath challah knife. Silver. 19th century. A very ornate knife showing the menorah and scenes from the Sabbath on its handle. *Private collection*.

Detail

Challah knife. Silver. Ludwig Wolpert. Just a half hour after this photograph was taken, we sat down and said the Sabbath blessings and cut the challah with this knife. *Nancy Berman and Alan Bloch Collection*.

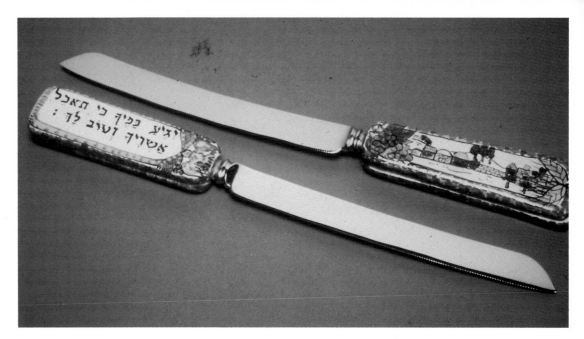

Two Challah knives, front and back. Painted wood. S. Kagan/I. Puski. *in the spirit gallery*. $150.

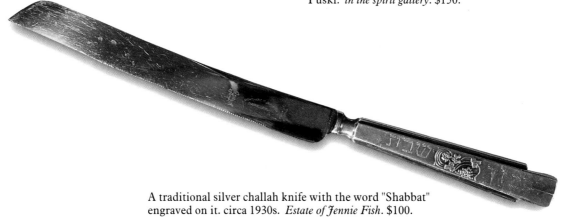

A traditional silver challah knife with the word "Shabbat" engraved on it. circa 1930s. *Estate of Jennie Fish*. $100.

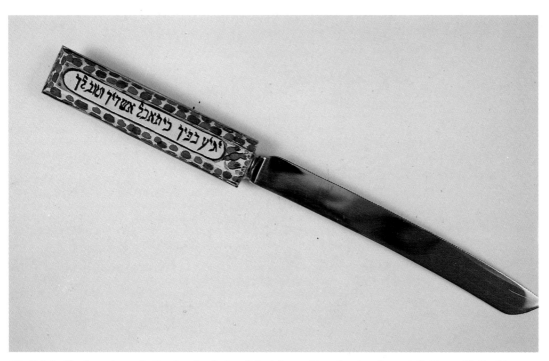

Challah knife. "...and yea shall enjoy the fruits of thy labors..." hand-painted wood. S. Kagan/ I. Puski. *in the spirit gallery*. $150.

Challah cloth. Woven textile. Peachy Levy. 1970s.

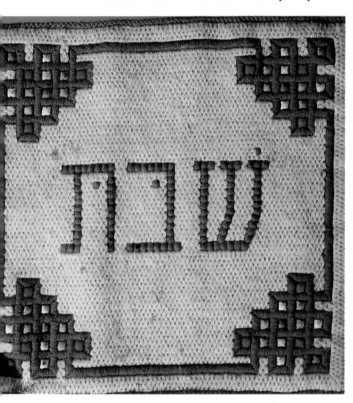

Challah cloth. Embroidered linen. Israel 1970s. *Collection of Caroline Goldfarb*. $30.

Above: Challah cloth. Needlepoint. 1970s. American. It is not unusual for wine spills to stain Jewish ceremonial linens. *Collection of Gabrielle Goldfarb*. $35.

Right: Shabbat platter. Brass and green patina. *Mrs. Lillian Altman Collection*. $100.

Chapter 2. Havdalah

Havdalah candle holders, havdalah wine cups, and spice boxes

The Havdalah service at the conclusion of the Sabbath has a lot of mystical significance. The word comes from the Hebrew word, "havdal" meaning separation since Havdalah separates the Sabbath from the rest of the week. The braided candle also shows symbolically how the Sabbath is part of the week and yet separate, and the spices remind one of the sweetness of the Sabbath.

Tradition says Havdalah begins when three stars are visible in the sky. It is then that the family gathers and the father says the blessing, holds up a special wine cup and then lights the intricately colored and braided Havdalah candle to signify the end of the Sabbath and the return to worldly activities.

"Blessed art Thou, O Lord our god, King of the Universe, Who made a distinction between light and darkness, between the holy and the ordinary, between the Sabbath and the weekday."

The spice box is passed around, the wine is sipped, the candle snuffed out in the wine, and the Sabbath is over.

Traditionally spice boxes often have been inspired by architecture and often resemble turreted medieval castles. Other spice boxes were designed in the shape of a fish because the fish had special significance in Jewish worship until the symbol was adopted by the early Christians. Spice boxes also come in the shape of flowers, acorns and other natural images.

Havdalah set. 20th century. S.Kagan. The braided Havdalah candle glows for a brief moment. The Sabbath is over. *in the spirit gallery.*

Havdalah candle holder. Nelles Studios. *in the spirit gallery.* $95.

Havdalah candle holders are usually wider than other candle sticks since the Havdalah candle is wider and holds more wicks. Since the havdalah candle is held during the blessing and then quickly extinguished, havdalah candle holders are smaller than the Sabbath candle sticks.

Jews were often among the poorer members of society until the late 19th century, and therefore most of them sought out cheaper materials such as pewter and brass for their ritual objects. Later it became more common to use brass and silver instead.

Havdalah candle holder. Silver. 1940s.
Ferne Kushner Collection. $250.

Spice container. Silver. Yehieh Yemini. Bezalel
School. 1920 Palestine. Yemini comes from a long
line of silversmiths. At age eight, he enrolled in
what was the first class at Bezalel and became a
student of Boris Schatz. *Private collection.*

Havdalah candle holder. Silver. 1940s.
Ferne Kushner Collection. $250.

In Hebrew Havdalah means separation and the
Havdalah ceremony separates the Sabbath from the rest
of the week. A braided Havdalah candle is lit when the
first star appears in the sky on Saturday evening. The
father says a blessing over the Havdalah wine cup and
takes a sip, and then passes around the Havdalah spice
box, "the besamin," dips the candle in the wine, and
the family is ready to return to their secular duties. The
Sabbath is over.

Havdalah spice box. Silver. 1940s. *Ferne Kushner Collection.* $250.

Havdalah spice box. 1860s. Brass. Engraved with the Havdalah prayer. This was carried by a traveling salesman who was an observant Jew and didn't want to miss the Havdalah service while traveling on the road. *Private collection*.

The other side.

ברוך אתה
יי אלהינו מלך
העולם בורא
מאורי האש

Inside the cover is the Havdalah prayer. The spices are stored on the other side. American. *Private collection*.

Spice boxes. Silver. Hungarian 19th century. Frequently spice boxes were modeled after turreted towers on European castles and palaces. *Congregation Keneseth Israel*. $500.

38

Havdalah candle holder. Silver. circa 1800 German. Bell trimmed 17th century spice box. 17th century silver filigree spice box. *Congregation Keneseth Israel*. $500.

Havdalah spice box. Silver filigree. 17th century European. *Congregation Keneseth Israel*. $500.

Havdalah spice boxes. *in the spirit gallery*. Silver fish. $500. Silver tower. $300. Silver tower with jewels. $500 and $300.

Havdalah spice container. Silver. 19th century central European. It was also common for spices to be stored in fish shaped containers. *Congregation Keneseth Israel*. $600.

39

The symbol of fish has been found on archeological sites in Israel. These mosaics were from a second century synagogue.

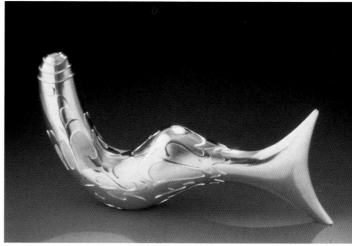

Spice Container. Silver: hammered, raised, applique and Florentine treatment. 5 1/2 X 11 1/4 in.., Moshe Zabari (b. 1935). 1994. "May God almighty bless you, make you fertile and numerous." Genesis 28:3. The fish shape was a messianic form used in many traditional spice containers. *Collection of the artist. Photography by D.R. Guthrie, Jerusalem.*

Havdalah Spice boxes. Silver. Eastern European. Late 1890s. *Rabbi Abraham Feldman Museum of the Congregation Beth Israel.*

Havdalah candle holders. Silver. 20th century. Havdalah candles are usually wider than traditional candles and are elaborately braided to symbolize the many aspects of life that are connected through the Sabbath and Havdalah services. *The National Museum of American Jewish History.* $200.

Havdalah Spice boxes. Silver. Spice boxes were often modeled on existing monuments and buildings and filled with architectural motifs and elements. *in the spirit gallery.* $200 and $500

Havdalah Spice box. Silver. Spice boxes come in many forms- birds, fish, flowers, windmills. 1900s. *Rabbi Abraham Feldman Museum of the Congregation Beth Israel.*

Havdalah spice boxes. Silver filigree. 20th century. *National Museum of American Jewish History*. $200.

Spice container. Silver, gold plated: hammered and raised. 9 5/8 X 5 in., Moshe Zabari (b. 1935). 1993. A sunflower shape is one of the many design motifs used in traditional spice containers. *Courtesy of Berenice and Sol Chadowitz, Edison, New Jersey. Photography by D.R. Guthrie, Jerusalem.*

Havdalah set. Silver. Bier. 20th century. *Rabbi Abraham Feldman Museum of the Congregation Beth Israel*. $1000.

Havdalah set. Silver/glass. 20th century. *Congregation Keneseth Israel.* $145.

Havdalah spice container. Silver. *The National Museum of American Jewish History.*

Havdalah candle holder. Silver. 20th century. 1970s. Israel. blessing. *Collection of Andrew Goldfarb.* $100.

Havdalah set. Pewter. Judith E. Goldstein. USA. "Heavenly Respite." The Kiddush cup is the Heavenly separation. The Besamin box is the Crescent moon embracing the three stars and the Havdalah candle holder is the crescent moon light. The design was inspired by the search of the heavens for the signs of the first three stars which signal the beginning of Havdalah. The separation of the Sabbath from the rest of the week is symbolized by the contrasting black and pewter surfaces. *Photography by Judith E. Goldstein.* $1800.

Above: Havdalah set. Pewter. Judith E. Goldstein. USA. 1991. "Starry Night." Again the artist makes references to the sighting of the three stars of Havdalah. The kiddush cup has one star. The candle holder has two and the besamin or spice box has three. The open cut star of David in the lid of the spice box allows the aroma of the spices to escape. *Photography by Judith E. Goldstein.* $3000.

Right:Detail

Havdalah set. Silver. Yaacov Greenvourcel. Israel. *in the spirit gallery.* $6500.

Havdalah set. Ebony/bronze/glass. L. Meiselman. *in the spirit gallery.* $2800.

Havdalah goblet and spice box. Ceramic. Robert Lipnick.
The National Museum of American Jewish History. $220.

Havdalah set. Ceramic. Robert Lipnick. *in the spirit gallery.* $895.

Havdalah set. Brass. dreidel/menorah. Brass. M. Shalem. Israel. *Brenda Bernstein collection.*

Chapter 3. Tzedakah

Tzedakah, the act of giving to others, is one of the basic precepts of Judaism. In the Talmud it is written "Tzedakah is equal to all the other commandments required." The word comes from the Hebrew word "Tzedek" which means justice.

Jews have always been assessed for "tzedakah" as a form of taxation and community responsibility. Even in the ancient Temple in Jerusalem there was a tzedakah box and contributions were not only used for Temple repairs and maintenance, but also for good deeds.

Tzedakah is not charity but acts of righteousness. In fact the translation of tzedakah is righteousness. And one of the earliest acts of tzedakah, say the rabbis, is Abraham's hospitality to the three strangers who came to his home. This act of righteousness is explained as another way that God tested Abraham's leadership of the Jews.

Today tzedakah is considered a part of the lives of most Jewish people and a part of many of the holiday traditions. Tzedakah is part of the Sabbath service as well as part of the High Holy Days and other holidays.

Traditionally tzedakah is collected before the candle lighting service on Sabbath. During the day before Yom Kippur, it is customary to remember the poor and give tzedakah as an offering on the eve of Yom Kippur. On Purim, Jews give "matanot laevyonim," gifts to the poor. On Passover Jews are exhorted to "let all who are hungry come and eat." And throughout the year it has become a custom for Jews to give thanks for special occasions such as births, bar/bat mitzvahs, anniversaries and deaths by giving tzedakah. Since the birth of Israel, contributing money to plant trees in Israel has become another form of Tzedakah.

In Yiddish a tzedakah box was called a "pushke." With the birth of the state of Israel, many Jewish homes would have a blue box, circulated by the Jewish National Fund and the United Jewish Appeal and the Joint Distribution Committee in which to place their tzedakah to further charitable causes in Israel.

Tzedakah boxes come in many shapes and styles. Throughout the late nineteenth and twentieth centuries, Jewish charities had their own small tin tzedakah boxes and Jews would send the filled boxes to the charity's headquarters. Traditional tzedakah boxes looked like metal banks with slots for coins. Other boxes were carved out of painted woods. Today tzedakah boxes come in silver, copper, brass and ceramic. Like the havdalah spice boxes, often tzedakah boxes make references to historic Jewish architecture.

Tzedakah bank. Tin. Early 20th century bank.
The National Museum of American Jewish History.

Alms Purse. Silver. Persia. Early 19th century. *Rabbi Abraham Feldman Museum of the Congregation Beth Israel.*

Often religious items had religious icons on one side and purely decorative elements on the other side. *Rabbi Abraham Feldman Museum of the Congregation Beth Israel.*

Alms box for Tzedakah. Wood. 1935. "Of Thine Own Have We Given Thee." *Rabbi Abraham Feldman Museum of the Congregation Beth Israel.*

Two silk ribbons given out at Hebrew charity events in 1882 and 1897. Until the twentieth century, Jews were often referred to as the Hebrew people. With the advent of Zionism in the late 1800s, many Jews chose to refer to themselves as lovers of Zion, using an old name, tzion, another name for Israel. *Private collection.* $50.

Tzedakah container. 1850. Painted Tin. The Roxbury Mutual Society. The slot has been added to the top of an ordinary tin can. *Private collection*.

Note the detail of the Hebrew letters which spell out the word tzedakah.

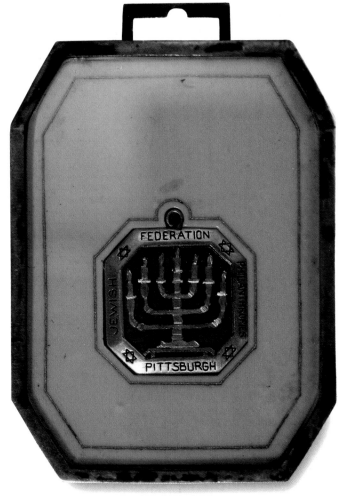

Tzedakah box. Silver. 20th century. Ari Solomon. Note the word tzedakah on the top of the container is supported by two lions of Judah. *in the spirit gallery*. $500.

Service Award. Silver. 1925 Jewish Federation Philanthropies of Pittsburgh service award to Abraham Oseroff. "in grateful recognition of his unselfish service during the campaign of 1925." *Private collection*. $25.

Tzedakah or righteous giving is one of the most importance mitzvot of Judaism. The giving of tzedakah comes before all the other commandments in the Torah.

Tzedakah is the act of good deeds and the act of giving to others. Jewish homes have always had a special box in which to place their coins for tzedakah to make giving a part of everyday life. In the late nineteenth and early twentieth century Jewish organizations would distribute tin charity boxes in which Jews could make contributions on a daily basis.

Gold and silver service pins given for philanthropic contributions. Clockwise. Leaf pin from the 1950s Baltimore. A 1970s silver pomegranate pin from the Jewish Federation of Allentown, Pennsylvania. A lion of Judah pin from Israel Bonds. A Jewish star pin given to the confirmation class of 1958 by Rabbi Abraham Feldman of Temple Beth Israel in West Hartford, Connecticut and a 1957 golden charm given to Jennie Fish on the occasion of her 50th wedding anniversary by her synagogue in Baltimore. Jennie and Max Fish had not only contributed money towards the building of the synagogue, but in the 1920s had rescued more than 100 Jews from their village in Poland and gave them train tickets to flee the pogroms and eventually emigrate to America. *Private collection.* $50 each.

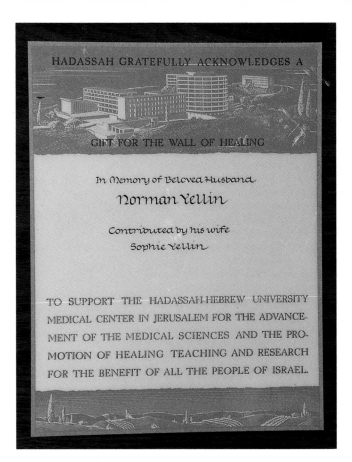

A certificate acknowledging a contribution to Hadassah Hospital in Jerusalem. *Private collection.* $50.

A certificate for 50 trees purchased in memory of Norman Yellin. Since the 1950s it has become customary for Jews to plant trees in Israel in memory or in honor of loved family and friends. *Private collection.* $50.

Tzedakah box from the Ladies Free Loan Association. American. Early 20th century. *Wilbur, Sara, and Paris Pierce Collection.* $500.

Left: "Pushe" or charity Box. Late 19th century. *Wilbur, Sara, and Paris Pierce Collection.* $300-500.

Above: Notice there is only a mention of Jerusalem and not Israel. Before the birth of Israel the Holy Land is referred to as Palestine or Jerusalem. After 1948, the land is referred to as Israel.

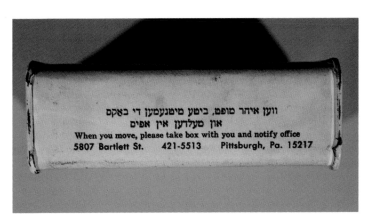

Left: Tzedakah box. Pre-1948 Israel. "In memory of the Sainted Grand Rabbi Josef Leifer...Pittsburgher Rebbe." In the early part of the 20th century some sects of American Jews retained a cult-like devotion to their "rebbe." *Wilbur, Sara, and Paris Pierce Collection.* $300-500.

Above: Detail

51

Tzedakah box. Post-1948 Israel. *Wilbur, Sara, and Paris Pierce Collection.* $300-500.

Notice that the blue box on the right has the name of the Jordanian city Aquaba written at the tip of the Red Sea thus dating it after the 1967 Six Day War. Blue Boxes. *Private collection.* $300-500.

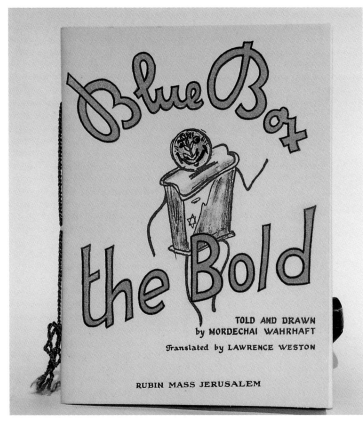

A rare early 20th century children's book printed in Jerusalem about a special hero, Blue Box the Bold. *Private collection.* $600-1000.

Detail

Blue Boxes. "Redeem the land of Israel" Blue Boxes were circulated by the Jewish National Fund from the 1920s and can be dated by the maps on the front. Note the map on the box to the left extends only to Hebron. All the names are in Hebrew letters whereas the blue box to the right is in English. The box on the left is a giant sized box. The other is the more common smaller sized box. *Private collection.* $300-500.

Tzedakah box. Federation of Jewish Philanthropies of New York. *Private collection.* $300-500.

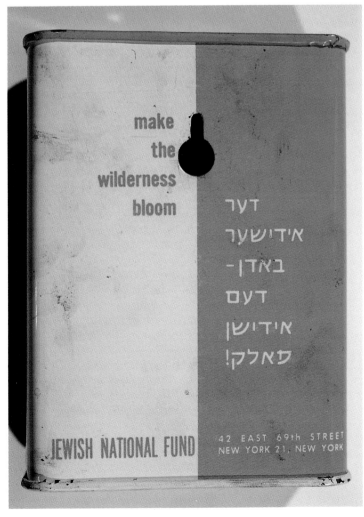

Above: Tzedakah boxes. Henry Street Settlement House and the Anti-Tuberculosis League of Palestine. *Private collection.* $300-500.

Right: The back of the blue box. "Make the wilderness bloom." Since the Jewish National Fund began to collect money in the late 1920s, Israel has reclaimed thousands of acres of swamp lands and unforested slopes and "made the desert bloom" and virtually eradicated malaria from the land of Israel.

Tzedakah box. Painted tin. Early 20th century. *Private collection.*

Tzedakah box. Sterling silver/bronze. Hana Geber. *in the spirit gallery.* $2400.

Tzedakah box. Silver. *in the spirit gallery.* $295.

Tzedakah box. Painted tin. *Private collection.* $300-600.

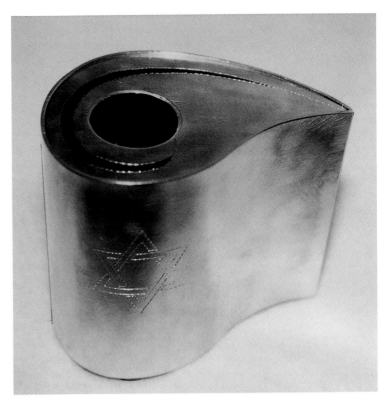

Tzedakah container. Pewter. "Spiraling Mitzvot." Judith E. Goldstein. USA. 1995. The giving of Tzedakah reinforces the spiritual quality of life in ever increasing spirals. *Photography by Judith E. Goldstein.* $300.

Tzedakah container. Pewter. "Deeds of Giving." Judith E. Goldstein. USA. 1994. Three is regarded as a special number and usually represents completeness and holiness. *Photography by Judith E. Goldstein.* $500.

Above: Tzedakah container. Silver. Moshe Zabari. *Nancy Berman and Alan Bloch Collection.*

Left: Tzedakah box. Sterling. Bier. Israel. *in the spirit gallery.* $395.

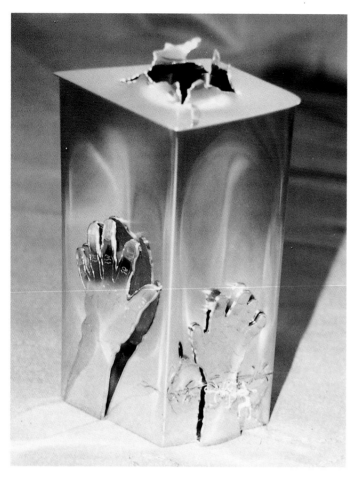

Tzedakah container. Pewter. Judith E. Goldstein. USA.
Photography by Judith E. Goldstein. Detail.

Tzedakah container. Pewter. Sterling silver. Black onyx beads.
Judith E. Goldstein. USA. "Reaching for Freedom." 1992. The
shape of the box with its shrunken sides and exploded top opening
sets the stage for this sculptural interpretation of tzedakah's role in
the struggle for freedom. The piece contrasts a free hand, growing
in strength, and a restrained hand, held down in barbed wire
shrinking to the bottom. *Photography by Judith E. Goldstein.* $3000.

Tzedakah container. Biran. *Audrey's at Skirball Cultural Center
and Museum.* $1200.

Tzedakah box. Silver. Ari Ofrir. *Audrey's at Skirball Cultural
Center and Museum.* $2000.

Tzedakah box. Ceramic. *Nancy Berman and Alan Bloch Collection.*

Tzedakah box. Zelig Segal. Israel. *Nancy Berman and Alan Bloch Collection.*

Above: Tzedakah box. Wood and inlay. Alex and Lorelei Gruss. *Private collection.*

Right: Tzedakah Box. Stained glass with a remnant of a piece of a 1906 Jewish greeting card. Leona Fein. USA. *The National Museum of American Jewish History.* $175.

Tzedakah box. Ceramic. Robert Lipnick. *The National Museum of American Jewish History*. $285.

Tzedakah box. Ceramic. Robert Lipnick. USA. The yellow keg lifts out and reveals the slot for coins. Lipnick, an Art History professor, is the son of a rabbi. *The National Museum of American Jewish History*. $425.

Above: Tzedakah box. Ceramic. Myra Kaplan. *The National Museum of American Jewish History*. $50.

Right: Tzedakah box. Hand-painted wood. B. Bernstein. M. Kalinovsky. *in the spirit gallery*. $250.

58

Tzedakah box. Ceramic. Garson/Pakele. USA. *in the spirit gallery.* $225.

Tzedakah box. Hand painted wood. Sticks. USA. Tzedakah is not considered charity by the Jews but a good deed and an act of righteousness on the part of the giver. *The National Museum of American Jewish History.* $450.

Above: Tzedakah box. Brass. B. Bernstein design. An original design based on Rachel's Tomb in Hebron. Rachel is one of the three biblical matriarchs- Sarah, Rebecca and Rachel. She married Jacob and became the mother of Joseph and his 10 brothers who became the leaders of the ten tribes of Israel. *in the spirit gallery.* $40.

Right: Tzedakah box. Hand-painted wood. S. Kagan/I. Puski. *in the spirit gallery.* $695.

Tzedakah boxes. Wood. Reuven Mazel. Israel. Like all other aspects of Judaica, synagogues have been built in many different styles and reflect popular period architecture. The Touro Synagogue in Newport, Rhode Island, the oldest in America, was founded by descendants of Marrano Jews and reflects the colonial style of Newport. Beth Sholom Synagogue in Elkins Park, Pennsylvania, was designed by Frank Lloyd Wright in modern style. Rodesh Sholom Synagogue, the second oldest congregation in Philadelphia, was founded in 1869 and reflects the popular Richardson style of the period. The oldest synagogue in Philadelphia, Mikveh Israel, is now part of The National Museum of American Jewish History. *The National Museum of American Jewish History.* $65 each.

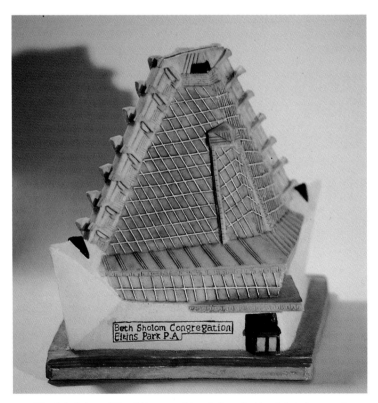

Tzedakah box. Wood. Reuven Mazel. Israel. Tzedakah boxes often refer to historic buildings like this modern mass-produced set of historic synagogues by Mazel in Israel. Beth Sholom synagogue in Elkins Park, Pennsylvania, was designed in 1958 by Frank Lloyd Wright. *The National Museum of American Jewish History.* $65.

Tzedakah box. Wood. Reuven Mazel. Israel. The Eldredge Street shul, which was founded in 1877, is the oldest congregation on New York's East Side. *The National Museum of American Jewish History.* $65.

Tzedakah box. Hand-painted wood. S. Kagan. *in the spirit gallery*. $495.

Tzedakah box. Hand-painted wood. S. Kagan. The Hamsa, or hand symbol because it looks like the letter "Shin," assumes the meaning of a divine blessing. *in the spirit gallery*. $495.

Tzedakah boxes. Wood. Shira. sterling/semi-precious stones. Hand painted wood. P. Gundling. *in the spirit gallery*. Sterling $195. wood $175.

Chapter 4. Mezuzah

A mezuzah is an enclosed container holding a parchment scroll on which is written the Shema, one of the most sacred prayers of the Jewish people. In this prayer (Deuteronomy (6:4-9; 11:13-21) God commands His People to hang this prayer on the doorposts of their homes. Mezuzah comes from the Hebrew word "doorpost." The letter "Shin" on top of each mezuzah is short for "*Shad dai,*" the anagram for the Hebrew letters "Shin," "Dalet," "Yud" which stand for *Shomer D'Latot Yisrael*...the guardian of the doorways of Israel.

During the Rosh Hashonah service, the congregation reads from the book of Deuteronomy which includes the most sacred prayer of the Jews, the Shema.

"Hear O Israel, the Lord Thy God, the Lord is one. You shall love thy Lord thy God with all thy heart, with all thy soul and with all thy might. And these commandments which I give you today shall be upon your heart. Thou shalt teach them diligently to your children, and shall speak of them when you sit in your home. When you walk by the way and when you lie down, and when you rise up. You shall bind them for a sign upon your hand, and they shall be as frontlets between thy eyes. You shall write them upon the doorposts of your home and your gates."

In this passage from Deuteronomy 6:4-9, God instructs His people on His laws and what He expects from them including placing a mezuzah on the "door posts of thy house and upon thy gates."

Today Jews follow this law by attaching a mezuzah, a small oblong container containing a piece of parchment on which are written the first few paragraphs of the Shema, the prayer found in Deuteronomy. "Hear O Israel, the Lord Thy God, the Lord is One." This parchment which must be written by a special scribe, a sofer, is then inserted into a hollow tube of wood, metal, silver, ceramic or glass and then fixed onto the doorpost of the house announcing to the world that this is a Jewish home. The mezuzah must be placed on the right hand side of the door, tilted towards the left, a third of the way down from the top.

Some Jewish families will place a mezuzah on every outside door and in every room of the house. Others just attach a mezuzah on one outside door. Mezuzahs are usually attached within thirty days of moving into a new home.

Traditionally mezuzahs were made out of wood and then later, metals such as brass and silver. Today mezuzahs are also made out of ceramics, Israeli stone, or glass. The traditional ones look more like architectural elements. Contemporary ones are more decorative.

Mezuzahs. Silver. Late 1890s and 1900s. *Rabbi Abraham Feldman Museum of the Congregation Beth Israel.*

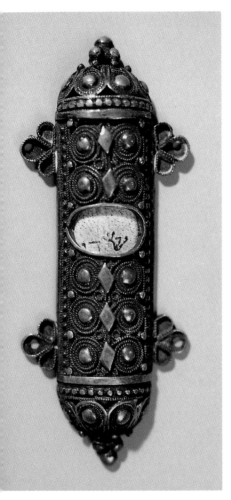

Above: Mezuzah. Silver. Bezalel School early 1900s. This mezuzah shows the early filigree style of the Syrian Jewish influence. It wouldn't be until the 1930s and 1940s when artists like Wolpert began to exert their influence that the school began to show modernistic trends in design. *Private collection.*

Above Center: In the 1900s there was a determined movement to make Hebrew the language of the Zionist movement and early Bezalel pieces were signed in Hebrew.

A Mezuzah is an enclosed container holding a parchment scroll on which is written the Shema, one of the most sacred prayers of the Jewish people. In Deuteronomy 6: 4-9 and 11:13-21, God commands His people to hang the Shema on the doorposts of their homes. "Mezuzah" comes from the Hebrew word "doorpost."

Mezuzah. Silver and Enamel. The Emanuel Winograd mezuzah depicts the twelve tribes of Israel and has the traditional Shin on top which is short for Shad dai.... the anagram for the Hebrew letters "Shin," "Dalet," "Yud" which stand for Shomer D'Latot Yisrael...the guardian of the doorways of Israel. *The National Museum of American Jewish History.* $1000.

Mezuzahs. Silver/copper. Barbara Wechsler Stemger. *The National Museum of American Jewish History*. $300

Mezuzah. Silver. 20th century. This mezuzah depicts the ark of the torah with a crown on top in place of the traditional symbol "Shin." *The National Museum of American Jewish History*.

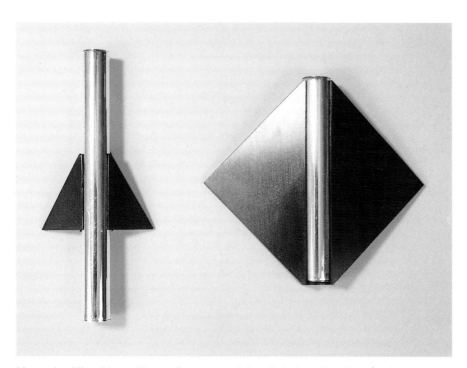

Mezuzahs. Silver/ebony. Yaacov Greenvourcel. Israel. *in the spirit gallery*. $295.

Mezuzah. Ivory/ebony/mahogany. Catriel. Israeli. The word "Shaddai" is written out. *in the spirit gallery*. $225.

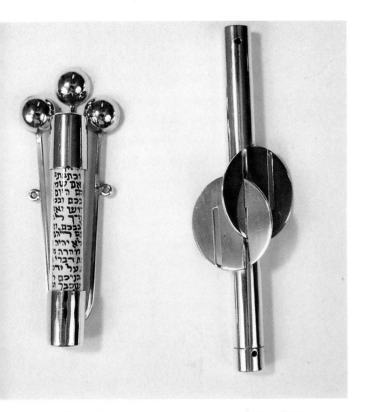

Mezuzahs. Silver. R. Landau. Israel. *in the spirit gallery*. $225 each.

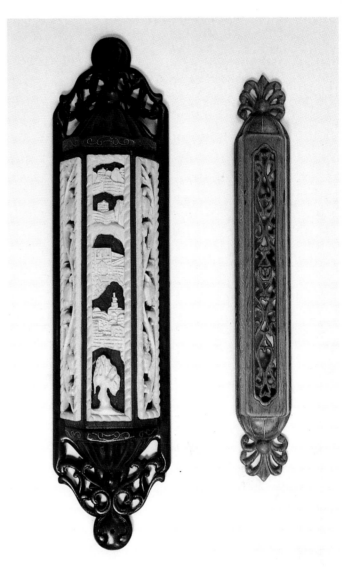

Mezuzahs. Hand-carved wood/ivory. Artist unknown. *in the spirit gallery*. $495 and $195.

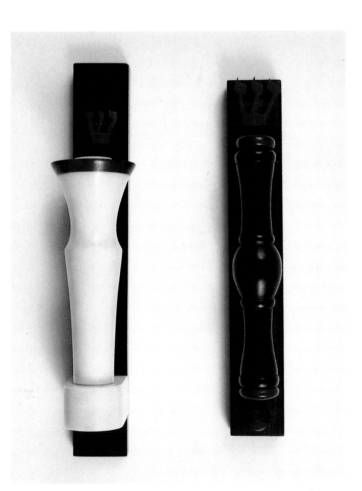

Mezuzahs. Hand-carved wood/ebony/alabaster. Dr. Robert Richter. USA. *in the spirit gallery*. $295.

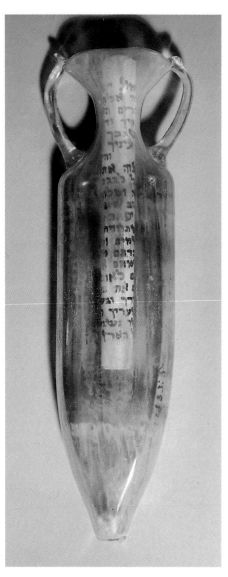

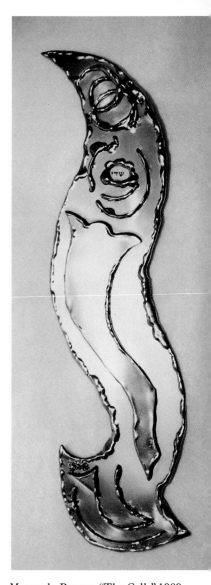

Mezuzah. Hand-blown glass. "The Space Shuttle" mezuzah. One of these mezuzot was taken into space in 1985 on the Fourth Discovery mission by astronaut Jeffrey Hoffman. This hand blown glass was based on the design of the container in which the Dead Sea Scrolls were found. The glass is indicative of the kinds of Roman glass found in archeological excavations in Israel. *in the spirit gallery.* $48.

Mezuzah. Handwrought non-tarnishing pewter. 1992. Judith E. Goldstein. USA. "A Blessing." "In ancient time the Kohanin, the priestly tribe of the Jews, blessed the people by stretching out their fingers-forming the letter `Shin,' the first initial of the Divine name. The cut out eye in the center suggested the rays of light radiating from Moses's head when he descended from Mt. Sinai. In Judaism the hand symbolizes Divine powers and protection, blessing and power. G-d re-deemed the Israelites from Egypt with a `strong hand.' Moses stretched forth his hand to split the Red Sea. Rabbis have been ordained by the laying on of hands. Parents lay their hands upon their children's heads to invoke G-d's blessing. The opening in the hand which reveals the Star of David is engraved in the shape of an eye. Tradition instructs us that G-d's eyes never close and so the eye is linked with Divine protection and power." *Photography by Judith E. Goldstein.* $125.

Mezuzah. Pewter. "The Call." 1989. Judith E. Goldstein. USA. *Photography by Judith E. Goldstein.* $135.

Mezuzah. Handwrought pewter with a sterling silver star and figure. "Seeking." Judith E. Goldstein. USA. 1993. *Collection Adam Goldstein. Photography by Judith E. Goldstein.* $135.

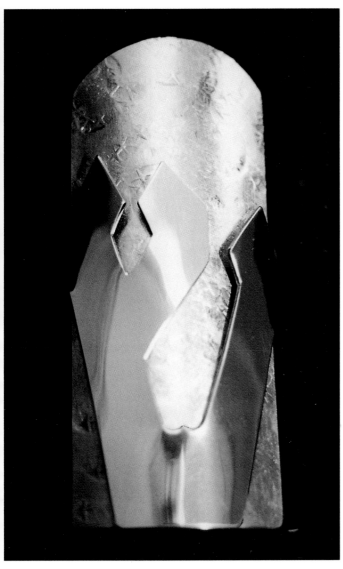

Mezuzah. Handwrought pewter. "Shin Shalom." 1996. Judith E. Goldstein. USA. The Hebrew letter Shin stands for "Shaddai" a divine name meaning Almighty. It is also an acronym for the "Guardian of Israel's Gates." *Photography by Judith E. Goldstein.* $150.

Mezuzah. Brass. Moshe Zabari. Israel. *Audrey's at the Skirball Cultural Center and Museum.* $650.

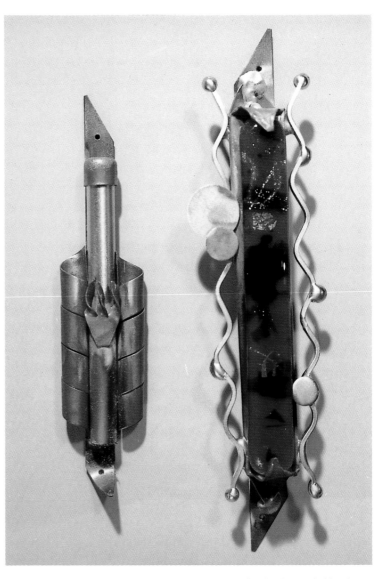

Mezuzah. Brass/enamel. Gary Rosenthal. USA. *in the spirit gallery.* $110.

Mezuzahs. Copper/glass/ brass/ steel. Gary Rosenthal. USA. Rosenthal has been sculpting in welded metals for over twenty years. A self taught artist he often incorporates a variety of materials to create unique designs. *Congregation Keneseth Israel.* $40-90.

Mezuzahs. John Wind. Pewter, gold, silver, jeweled and Austrian crystal. These mezuzahs are based on the imagery and designs of Chagall. *The National Museum of American Jewish History.* $200.

Mezuzah. Hand-painted wood/Plexiglas, parchment. B. Bernstein design. *in the spirit gallery.* $195.

Mezuzah. Brass/glass. Gary Rosenthal. U.S.A. Notice the stylized "Shin." *Congregation Keneseth Israel.* $90.

Right: Mezuzah. Hand painted wood/parchment/plexiglass. S. Kagan/I. Puski. *in the spirit gallery.* $185.

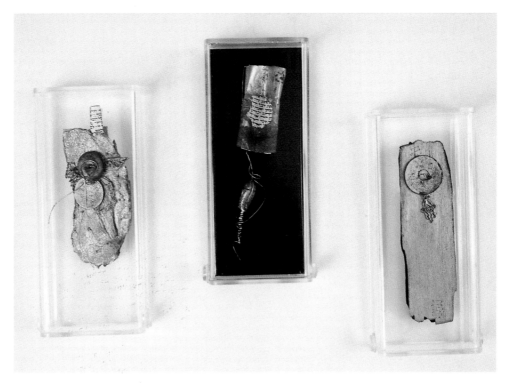

Mezuzahs. Found object with parchment. J. Zimmerman. *in the spirit gallery*. $195.

Mezuzahs. Enamel/bronze. K. Rossi. *in the spirit gallery*. $120.

Mezuzah. Ceramic. Chaya Magal. 20th century. Israeli folk artist. *Edythe Siegel Gallery of American-Jewish Folk Art*. $75.

Mezuzahs. Ceramic. Robert Lipnick. USA. *The National Museum of American Jewish History.* $230.

Mezuzah. Hand-painted. *in the spirit gallery.*

Mezuzahs. Ceramic. H. Miller. *in the spirit gallery.* $150-175.

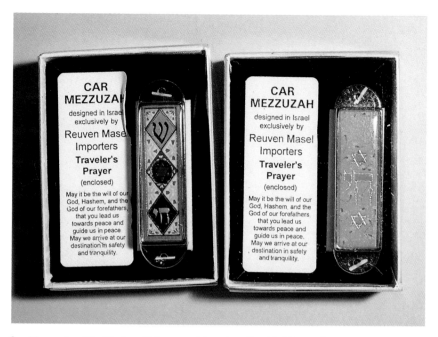

Car Mezuzahs. *The National Museum of American Jewish History.* $15.

Mezuzah. Woven. Peachy Levy.

Mezuzahs. Metal/green paint. Israel. *Congregation Keneseth Israel.* $6

Chapter 5. Rosh Hashonah and Yom Kippur
The High Holy Days

Shofars, Torah covers, Torah crowns, Torah finials, yads, kipahs, tallit, and New Year's Cards

Why is the Jewish New Year, Rosh Hashonah, a holy day and not a holiday? Unlike the secular New Year, when Jews and non-Jews celebrate *life*, Jews at their New Year take time out for solemn reflection about *death*. During the year, Jews joyously toast 'l'Chaim,' to life, but on Yom Kippur they turn introspective and recall the lives of those who have died in previous years, and re-examine their own lives. What if this was to be their last year on earth?

Is dwelling on thoughts about the dead during these particular days morbid? No, it is more about affirming quality of life. As Jews sit in services, the rabbis tell them

New Year card. 1900s. Germany.

that the names of those who will live and those who will die during the coming year have already been written in the book of life. It is then that Jews think about their own mortality, and unlike the secular New Year's Eve resolutions to lose weight, eat less, drink less, exercise more, spend more time with their children, parents, husbands, Jews worry how their lives will be judged and remembered after they are gone.

Perhaps it is a sense of superstition that at the thought of death, Jews decide to atone for their sins, pray, fast and hope for a clean slate. Perhaps it's a sense of reality. If you have just one year left, there is a moral obligation to make it your best and if it is going to be your last, what does money and weight loss really matter?

Many Jews celebrate the holy days by visiting the cemeteries and making a pilgrimage to their past and pay homage to the dead by leaving stones on top of the graves to show that the dead have not been forgotten.

"In the seventh month, in the first day of the month, shall be a solemn rest unto you, a memorial proclaimed with the blast of the horns, a holy gathering."

Rosh Hashonah and Yom Kippur are called the Days of Awe and are considered the two most solemn of the Jewish holidays. During the two days of Rosh Hashonah and the one day of Yom Kippur, Jews stay home from work and attend services at their synagogues and temples. Yom Kippur, the tenth day of Tishri and the most solemn of the holy days is called the Day of Atonement and Jews are required to fast for twenty-four hours.

Since Jewish holidays are celebrated according to the Hebrew calendar, the dates of observance vary each year. Although Rosh Hashonah and Yom Kippur occur on the first ten days of Tishri, the seventh month of the Hebrew year, Rosh Hashonah, means the beginning of the New Year. The first month of the year used to be Nisan which occurs in the spring, but since ancient Israel was an agricultural society and the harvests became more important to the economy, Tishri which marked the end of the harvest, became the beginning of the economic year and before long all the business dealings, contracts, sabbatical years and jubilees began on the first of Tishri.

The most common objects associated with Rosh Hashonah and Yom Kippur are the Torah and the Shofar. In Exodus when the Lord gives Moses the Ten Commandments, He also instructs him in how to design a beautiful

Jewish synagogue key from Manheim, Germany, 1851. *Rabbi Abraham Feldman Museum of the Congregation Beth Israel.*

ark, an ark cover, a Torah crown and a Torah mantle. Since then it has become customary to build an ornate and decorative wooden ark in which to store the Torah, design an ornate silver crown for the Torah, a silver breastplate or amulet to hang over the Torah and a silk or elaborately embroidered cover for the scroll.

The Torah is wrapped around two rods of wood called "rimmonim" which is also the word for pomegranates. Both the Torah crowns and Torah finials are usually made of precious metals, jewels and semi-precious stones and often resemble the crowns and orbs of power of royalty. It has been said that medieval Torah crowns were inspired by the crowns worn by Madonnas in Baroque paintings and European royalty. Torah coverings which are usually embroidered silk or velvet cases resemble the priestly robes and royal gowns. Arks tended to reflect the elaborate altarpieces often found in the Christian churches of Europe.

Since the Torah, the Old Testament, is the five books of Moses and a sacred and holy book, it must not be touched and soiled by human hands. A new portion is read every week and as the rabbi reads the Torah in front of the congregation he gives "aliyahs" to selected members of the congregation sharing with them the honor and privilege of assisting him in reading.

Readers of the Torah use a "Yad," or Torah pointer made out of wood, bone, silver, gold or ivory to follow along with the text. The Hebrew word "yad" means finger and it has become traditional for yads to look like a finger pointing towards the sacred text.

The Torah says that the rabbis must wear special priestly robes, shoes and silver buckles during the High Holidays. Many rabbis today wear special white robes and

special shoes. Yom Kippur belt buckles are some of the unusual objects that have become highly prized today.

On the High Holy days of Rosh Hashonah and Yom Kippur the rabbi and his congregation open the Torah and read Genesis, Bereshish...In the beginning... the story of Adam and Eve. On Rosh Hashonah one reads the story of the sacrifice of Isaac and the story of Esau and Abel.

The shofar, the ram's horn, sounded on the High Holy days to awaken the souls of worshipers to rethink their lives and goals for the coming year, is one of the most visible symbols of the High Holidays. The shofar, which was originally a primitive musical instrument, is sounded during the Rosh Hashonah service and at the conclusion of the Yom Kippur service. Today the shofar has become a symbol of God calling his people together to atone for their sins. The ram's horn also reminds us of the intended sacrifice of Isaac by Abraham and the fact that when God intervened and sent a ram to be sacrificed in his place, he saved Isaac's life.

There are four different sequences of notes blown on the shofar: 1) tekiah, a long and sustained sound; 2) shebarim, three broken notes; 3) teruah, nine short series of notes; and 4) tekiah, the long unbroken sustained sound and the final sound, which is a combination of the other three. Rabbis and sages have attributed many mystical interpretations to these sounds and rhythms.

Usually the shofar is made from a ram's horn that has been boiled in water until it gets soft. Then the inside is hollowed out and the horn is somewhat flattened, the mouth piece is carefully shaped and the horn is put aside to harden again. Shofars can have a soft curve, be elongated or have a very pronounced curve. Surfaces can be smooth or heavily carved with designs and Hebrew calligraphy.

During the Rosh Hashonah meal it has become the tradition to dip apples in honey and recite this blessing "May God grant us a good and sweet year."

Kipahs are the traditional skull caps worn by Orthodox and Conservative male Jews to show reverence for God and acknowledgment of His presence. While kipah is the twentieth century usage, years ago these small cloth skull caps were better known by their Yiddish or Jewish name, *yarmulke,* or simply skull caps. Traditionally they were made from black silk. Today they come in all colors and are embriodered with names, stars, and other decorative symbols. But while their name, color, and design have changed, their purpose remains constant and kipahs are respectful outward signs of man's piety and humility in the presence of God.

The Mogen David, or Star of David, is the most widely seen symbol of both the Jewish people and the Jewish state. Originally it became a symbol to ward off demons and evil spirits, but in 1897 it was adopted by the first Zionist Congress as its emblem, and later became the central motif of the Israeli flag.

New Year card. 1900s. American. Three dimensional cards were popular at the turn of the century in America and in Europe. *Private collection.* $250

New Year card. 1900s. American. Three dimensional cards were popular at the turn of the century in America and in Europe. *Private collection.* $250.

New Year card. 1900s. American. Popular turn of the century New Year card. *Private collection.* $250.

A Tashlik scene. "Casting your sins upon the waters." Hand painted wood. M. Kasinofsky. Russian. A week before the High Holidays, it is the custom for Jews go to the river to wash away their sins. *in the spirit gallery.* $325.

Honey dish. Hand painted porcelain. "May He renew us for a good and sweet year." *in the spirit gallery.* $150.

Round Challah plate. Pewter, colorized pewter, ebony, garnet, peridot, Swarovski crystal, black onyx, gold. Judith E. Goldstein. USA. "In the Beginning." 1990. This dish, which was designed to hold the ceremonial round challah bread only baked during the High Holidays, shows the seven days of creation. *Photography by Judith E. Goldstein.* $4000.

Honey Dish set. Silver. Michael Strauss. *Audrey's at the Skirball Cultural Center and Museum.* $1500.

Torah belt. Silver and velvet. 19th century. *Rabbi Abraham Feldman Museum of the Congregation Beth Israel.*

On the High Holy days of Rosh Hashonah and Yom Kippur the rabbi and his congregation open the Torah and read Genesis, "Bereshish"...in the beginning—the story of Adam and Eve. On Rosh Hashonah one reads the story of the sacrifice of Isaac and the story of Esau and Abel. The shofar is an important part of the High Holy Days observance. God commanded Bezalel to make a beautiful ark, covers and adornments for the Torah. The staves of the Torah's scroll are adorned with finials, a crown is placed on top, a shield or breast plate hangs from the staves, and a silk or satin mantle covers the entire Torah which, when not in use, is stored in the ark, a cabinet set against the central wall of the synagogue.

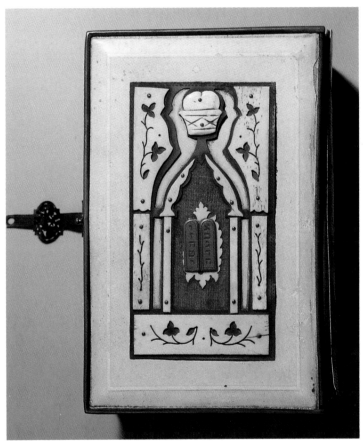

Above: Prayerbook. Ivory. Brass. This prayerbook was owned by Leah Title and printed in Vienna in 1893. *Rabbi Abraham Feldman Museum of the Congregation Beth Israel.*

Left: Prayerbook. Ivory, brass. 1850s. This was the prayerbook of the first president of Congregation Beth Israel in West Hartford, Connecticut. Since most Jews came from Europe and could speak German and English, (Yiddish is a form of German-Jewish), many of the earliest prayer books, like this were printed in German and English. This book was printed in Vienna in 1857 and was owned by a Meyer Stein. *Rabbi Abraham Feldman Museum of the Congregation Beth Israel.*

Belt Buckle to be worn only on Yom Kippur. Silver repousse. Myer Myers. 1760. Myers was one of the leading silversmiths of colonial times and one of the most famous Jewish craftsmen. *Rabbi Abraham Feldman Museum of the Congregation Beth Israel.*

Yom Kippur belt buckle. Silver. Polish. 19th century. "For on that day should the priest make an atonement for you to cleanse you that you may be clean of all your sins before the Lord. For on this day he will purify you from all your sins and you shall be purified before the Lord." Inscription written on the back. *Rabbi Abraham Feldman Museum of the Congregation Beth Israel.*

Torah Crown. Silver. *Rabbi Abraham Feldman Museum of the Congregation Beth Israel.*

Torah Breast Plate. Silver. Torah Breast plate from Nurenberg, Germany dated 1783. The shield shows the lions of Judah and the Ten Commandments as well as a Torah crown.

Buckle. Silver. *Rabbi Abraham Feldman Museum of the Congregation Beth Israel.*

Above: Torah finials. Silver. Note the dove of peace on the top. 19th century. *Rabbi Abraham Feldman Museum of the Congregation Beth Israel.*

Left: Torah finials. Brass. Tunisian. Twentieth century. *Private collection.*

Torah Crown. 19th century. *Rabbi Abraham Feldman Museum of the Congregation Beth Israel.*

Maquette of a synagogue ark designed for the synagogue in White Meadow, New Jersey. *in the spirit gallery.*

Above: The Holy Scriptures. Satin cover. Given out as a gift to the girls in the 1958 confirmation class of Temple Beth Israel, West Hartford, Connecticut. *Private collection.* $45.

Right: Torah bookends. Carved wood. 1950s. Best student award in the fifth grade Sunday School class of the Emanuel Synagogue. Hartford, Connecticut. *Private collection.* $30.

Eternal light. Silver/turquoise. 17th century European. A hanging lamp with an eternal flame or light is hung over the ark of the Torah in every synagogue and temple to indicate that God is always present. *Congregation Keneseth Israel.*

Two 19th century Viennese silver repousse silver Torah finials with bells Buchara 19th century. *Congregation Keneseth Israel.*

Two 17th century Yemenite silver filigreed Torah finials. *Congregation Keneseth Israel.*

Torah crown. Silver. 18th century. *Congregation Keneseth Israel.*

Tallis. Embroidered silk.

Tallit or prayer shawls hang outside Jewish synagogues.

An 18th century leather covered prayer book.
Congregation Keneseth Israel.

The inside pages reveal hand written Hebrew still intellegible today.

Bible book cover. Antique/gold, silver, semi-precious stones. *in the spirit gallery.* $900.

Torah cover. Paper. Signed and numbered. Agam. Israel. *in the spirit gallery.* $1200.

Scribes box. Brass. Oriental. circa 1850. *in the spirit gallery.* $2400.

Kipahs. Velvet. Gold and silver threads. Orthodox Jewish males wear a head covering called a yarmulke (Yiddish) or a Kipah (Hebrew) whenever they are in the presence of God. While some only wear one in a synagogue, others wear them everyday because they believe that God is everywhere. Conservative Jewish males wear kipahs in the synagogue. Reform Jews generally don't wear a kipah in temple. *The National Museum of American Jewish History.* $12.

Kipahs. Leather. *The National Museum of American Jewish History*. $18.

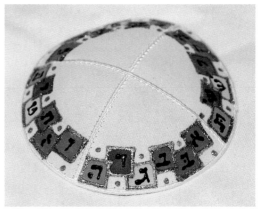

Kipah. Leather and gold and silver threads. Young boys like to choose more colorful kipahs. *The National Museum of American Jewish History*. $18.

Kipahs. Woven Yarn. For years kipahs were skull caps and were traditionally made out of black rayon. But beginning in the 1970s, colored silk and satin kipahs became popular as Bar Mitzvah favors. Today kipahs come in different colors and materials. This smaller knitted kipah seems to lie best on the head although some men still keep their kipah in place with a hair pin. *The National Museum of American Jewish History*. $15.

Torah container. Olivewood. Olivewood objects have been popular souvenirs of the Holy Land since the late 19th century. *Private collection.* $150.

Detail

Woven cover. Peachy Levy. "Therefore Choose Life. " These words came from Moses' last speech. It refers to living life according to Law and according to the Mitzvot. Torah finials are called rimmonim because they look like pomegranates. Pomegranates were ancient symbols embroidered on the hems of the High Priests in the Bible. Tradition says that the pomegranates have 613 seeds, the same number of mitzvot required in the Torah. Therefore pomegranates have come to symbolize tzedakah.

Tallis, tallis bag, Israeli kipah. Woven. Gert Zuckerman. 1971. *Alexander Goldfarb collection.*

85

Since the Torah is a sacred item and made of perishable parchment, it should not be touched on a daily basis by human hands. Therefore, Torah readers use a pointer made of wood, ivory, bone or precious metals called a Yad, or finger, to follow along with the text. "Yad" is the Hebrew word for "finger."

Yad. Silver. 18th century Italian gloved Torah pointer. 15th century Viennese Torah pointer. Silver. Yad means a finger. It is against the law to touch the Torah with a bare hand. So it became a tradition to use a metal pointer often shaped in the shape of a finger. These are more elaborate in their costuming than most. *Congregation Keneseth Israel.*

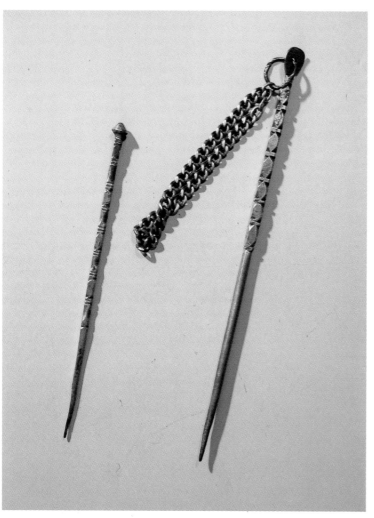

Yads. Silver. 18th century. Germany. *Congregation Keneseth Israel.*

Yad. Engraved silver. 18th century. The words say "Moses is true and His Torah is True." *Congregation Keneseth Israel.*

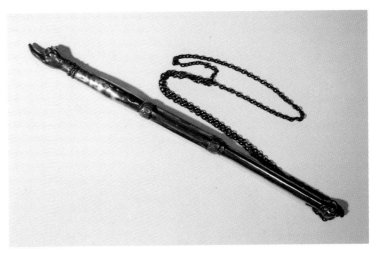

Yad. Silver. Eastern European, probably Poland. Circa 1860s. Presented to the Congregation on September 14, 1867. *Rabbi Abraham Feldman Museum of the Congregation Beth Israel.*

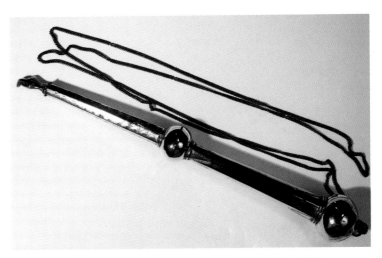

Yad. Carved Ivory/semi-precious stones. L. Persian circa 1900. $3200. 20th century reproduction. bone. *in the spirit gallery.* $50.

Yad. Silver. Eastern European. Circa 1870s. *Rabbi Abraham Feldman Museum of the Congregation Beth Israel.*

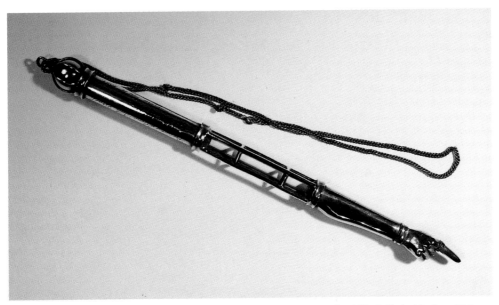

Yad. 1849. Silver. Poland. Three sections with a crown on its orb. There should be balls inside the middle section to ward off evil. This yad was a gift from Alexander Rothschild to the congregation in 1849. Rothschild was one of the founders of Beth Israel. *Rabbi Abraham Feldman Museum of the Congregation Beth Israel.*

Yad. Embossed silver with a bird on top. The cuff is separate.
Rabbi Abraham Feldman Museum of the Congregation Beth Israel.

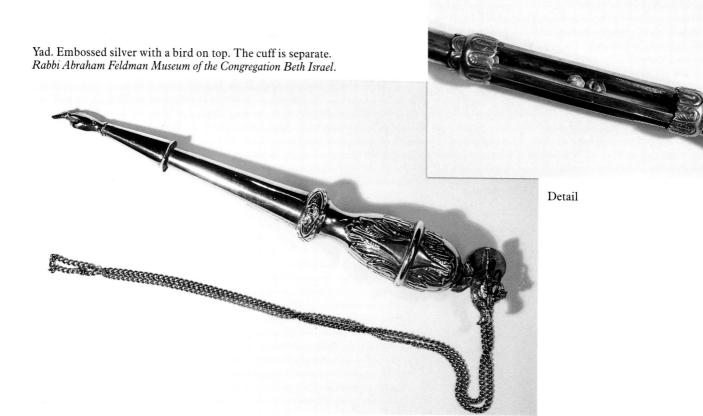

Detail

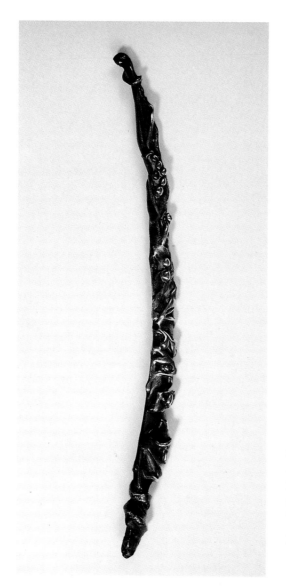

Above: Yad. Pewter. Silver Torah. "May You ever Reach Toward Torah's Wisdom." 1996. Judith E. Goldstein. USA. This design was inspired by the artist's daughter Jordana who asked her mother to design a yad for her Bat Mitzvah that looked like a hand. The Torah ring creates the symbolism of a hand reaching towards Torah. *Photography by Judith E. Goldstein.* $100.

Left: Yad. Sterling/bronze. Hana Geber. *in the spirit gallery.* $1800.

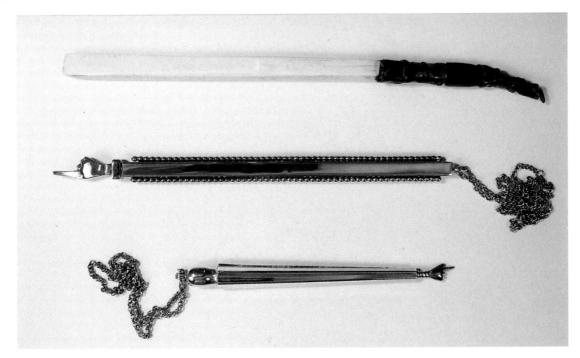

Yads. *in the spirit gallery*. Top: Sterling. $160. Middle: Sterling $295. Bottom: Silver/ivory. S. Kagan. $1800.

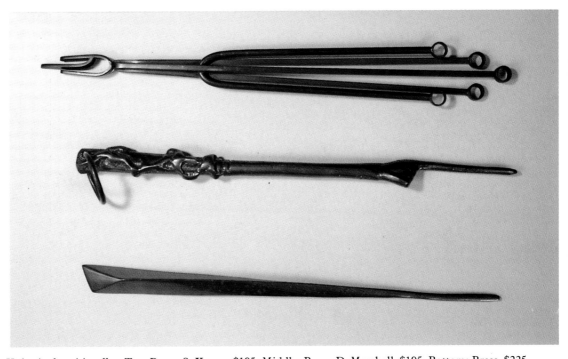

Yads. *in the spirit gallery*. Top: Brass. S. Kagan. $195. Middle: Brass. D. Marshall. $195. Bottom: Brass. $225.

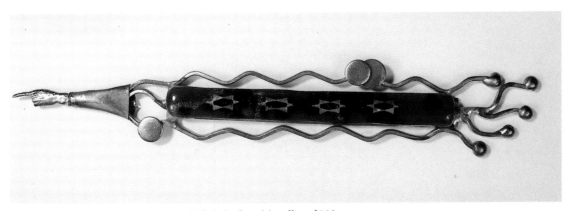

Yad. Brass/enamel. Gary Rosenthal. *U.S.A. in the spirit gallery*. $110.

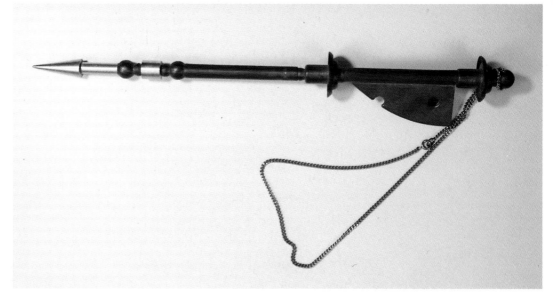

Yad. Brass. *in the spirit gallery*.

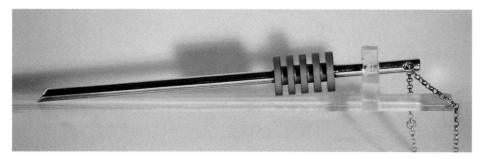

Yad. Sterling silver/ titanium. Rati Landau. *in the spirit gallery*. $185

The shofar, or ram's horn, sounded on the High Holy days awakens the souls of worshipers to rethink their lives and goals for the coming year. "Awake, ye sleepers," ....begins the call to worship for Rosh Hashonah, and the shofar is sounded to make man rethink his goals and his ideals, and make the next year "l'shana tova..." a good new year.

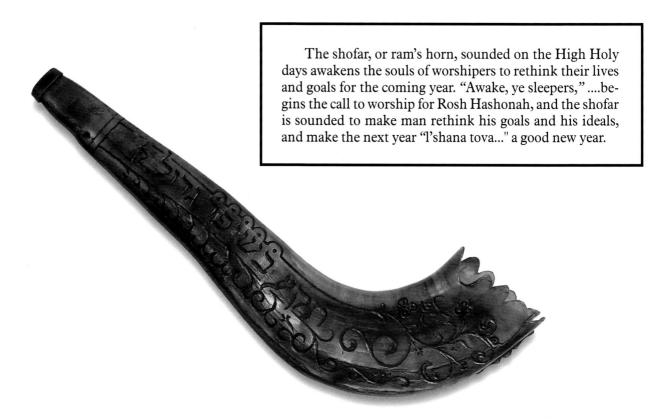

Shofar. Polish. 1828. Etched designs of flowers and scroll foliage. Inscribed on one side with the Hebrew text, "Praise Ye God with the blowing of the shofar." On the other side it says "Blow the great shofar, blow with a trumpet-like sound." *Rabbi Abraham Feldman Museum of the Congregation Beth Israel*.

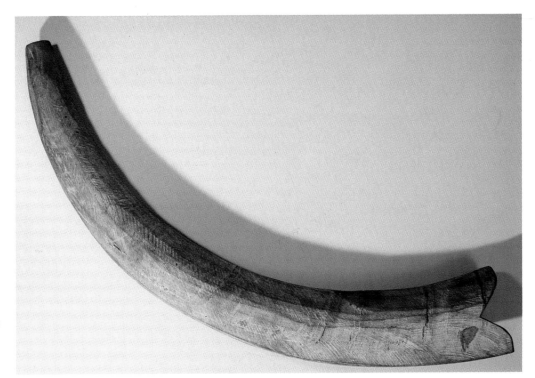

Shofar. 18th century. bone. *Congregation Keneseth Israel*.

Shofar. Black. 20th century. $36.

Shofar. Extra Large. 20th century. *The National Museum of American Jewish History*. $200.

Two 19th century ram horns.
Congregation Keneseth Israel.

Shofar. This shofar was bought in Israel from a
Moroccan. The collector said that she bought it
"because it was unpolished and still had the look of
the animal." *Private collection.*

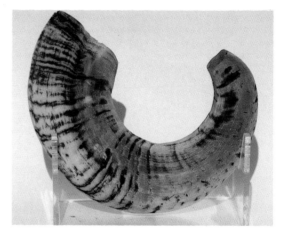

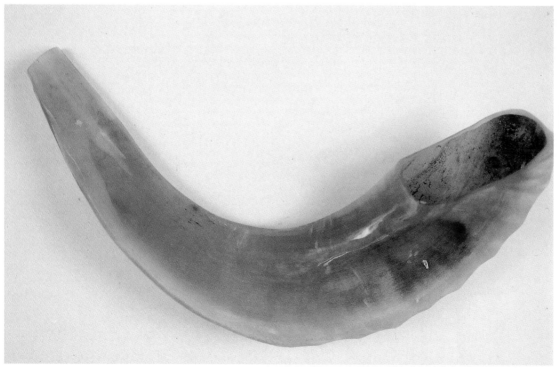

Shofar. Ram's horn. 20th
century. *in the spirit gallery.* $95.

Chapter 6. Succoth
Estrog boxes, lulav holders, and mizpahs

One of the rewards of fasting on Yom Kippur is the fact that after the fast is broken, Jews begin preparations to build a Sukkah, a three-sided temporary shelter that recalls the agricultural shelters inhabited by the ancient Israelites and five days later they begin the week long celebration of Succoth, the biblical harvest feast of the Jews.

The first mention of Succoth is in the Bible when God commanded the Israelites in Exodus 23: 14-16 to remember Him three times a year with a celebration...the feast of the unleavened bread, Passover; the feast of the harvest, Shavuot; and the feast of Ingathering, Succoth.

According to the Bible, "You shall dwell in booths for seven days..So that your generations may know that I made the children of Israel to dwell in booths when I brought them out of Egypt."

The law further says that the sukkah must have an open roof to see the stars above, be open on the fourth side to be closer to nature, and to further emphasize its temporary nature, the Sukkah must not be fastened with any nails. It is taught that the holiday of Succoth is one of the most democratic of the Jewish holidays because both the rich and the poor shall live in these open huts and for

An early 19th century sukkah from southern Germany with a landscape of Jerusalem painted in the background. This is now on permanent display in the Israel Museum in Jerusalem.

the seven days of Succoth, neither the poor nor the rich will fare better than the other.

Often called the Feast of the Tabernacles, or the Feast of the Booths, or the Feast of the Ingathering, Succoth is also called the Jewish Thanksgiving since like the American secular holiday, it also celebrates the end of the harvest. In fact, it has been said that the Pilgrims and the American founding fathers modelled their Thanksgiving celebrations on this ancient Jewish religious festival.

Jewish historians trace the origin of Succoth to an ancient Canaanite festival which was held after the grape harvests to encourage rain.

In both America and in Israel, the holiday is characterized by joyous celebrations and parties while the family decorates the hut with fruits and vegetables. And during the holiday, families eat in their Sukkah and recite a series of prayers using four symbols: an "estrog," a round yellow citron; and a "lulav," a palm branch which is wrapped with the leaves from both the "aravah," the willow, and the "hadassah," the myrtle tree.

Like most Jewish ceremonial items, the lulav and the estrog have philosophical meanings. The ancient rabbis spent many hours discussing and trying to interpret the words and meanings of each law. And through the centuries, they have handed down a mystical interpretation of the symbolism of the lulav and the estrog.

The rabbis say that the four components of the lulav and estrog which are called in Hebrew, the "arba minim," symbolize the human condition and man's relationship with God.

The estrog is shaped like the heart of man. The lulav is the spine. The myrtle leaves are shaped like the eyes and the willow leaves are shaped like the lips. Together these four elements show that man should serve the Lord thy God with his heart, his spine or body, his eyes and his lips.

There is another symbolic element that relates to "learning" which is prized among the Jews, and "tzedakah" which is good deeds. The estrog which has a good taste and a good smell, is like those Jews who know the law and do good deeds. While the lulav which has a good taste, but no smell, is like a person with knowledge who does no good deeds. The myrtle which has a good smell and no taste is like a simple person who has no knowledge and learning but is innately kind and caring. Lowest on the rung of human values is the willow which has neither taste nor fragrance and symbolizes those people with no interest in gaining knowledge and no innate sense of responsibility towards others and no feeling of the need to help others through tzedakah or good deeds.

Each day during Sukkoth, blessings are recited over the estrog and the lulav. The estrog must be held in the left hand and the lulav in the right hand. Then the lulav is shaken in the four directions to remind the Jews that God is everywhere.

Among those objects used in the Succoth service is the box used to store the estrog and an embroidered case in which to carry the lulav. Since Orthodox Jews believe that an estrog must be perfect and without flaws, estrogs are carried to services in an estrog box in which there is usually a cushion of soft material such as horse hair.

Traditional estrog boxes are usually in the shape of the fruit itself. Early estrog boxes were adapted from silver sugar bowls, soap dishes and other silver containers. In the late 19th century many tourists brought back olivewood estrog boxes from the Holy Land. Today most estrog containers are either silver, pewter or ceramic. Many families allow the estrog to wither and save it for the next year in the estrog box.

Lulavs are carried to services in a lulav carrier which is either a velvet embroidered case with the words of the prayer embroidered on its sleeve.

Often Jews who lives in the Western world will hang a Mizrah, a wooden plaque on the eastern wall of the sukkah facing towards Jerusalem to remind them of the temple in Israel. Jews who live in Iraq, Singapore, India, China etc., hang their mizpahs on the western wall.

In Israel, it is not unusual to see small makeshift shacks appear throughout the Orthodox neighborhoods. In America, while many families build their own sukkahs, more prefer to enjoy the sukkahs built by their synagogues. It is traditional for young Jewish children to attend sukkah parties at Sunday school and help decorate the sukkahs with fall fruits, vegetables and corn stalks. Orthodox families traditionally have open houses and parties to share their sukkahs with friends.

Estrog box. Silver. *in the spirit gallery.*

Sukkahs in the Mea Shearim neighborhood of Jerusalem. During the eight days of Succoth, Jews build a sukkah, a temporary outdoor hut, say blessings over an estrog and lulav, and serve and eat their meals in their sukkah. Traditional ceremonial items are an estrog box to store and carry the estrog, a lulav carrier to store and carry the lulav and usually a plaque to decorate the inside of the sukkah.

Estrog box. Tin. A scene showing the prayers over the lulav and the estrog.

Etrog and Lulav holder. Silver, pierced and formed. Moshe Zabari (b. 1935). 1992. "product of goodly trees, branches of palm trees, boughs of leafy trees and willows of the brook.." Leviticus 23:40. This is a combined holder for the four species of plants- the palm, myrtle, the willow, and the etrog. *Collection of the artist. Photography by D.R. Guthrie.*

95

Estrog Box. Silver. *in the spirit gallery.*

Above: Estrog containers. 1900s. Silver. *Rabbi Abraham Feldman Museum of the Congregation Beth Israel.*

Right: Estrog container. Painted metal. Israel. 1940s. *Private collection.*

Estrog container. Painted cast metal. 20th-century
Israeli egg shaped. *Rabbi Abraham Feldman Museum
of the Congregation Beth Israel.*

Estrog box. Olivewood. Late 19th or early 20th century. *Private collection.*

Estrog box. Carved olivewood circa 1850. *Rabbi Abraham Feldman Museum of the Congregation Beth Israel.*

Estrog box. Silver. Orthodox Jews will not accept an estrog with a blemish so they carry the estrog back and forth from services in an estrog container. *The National Museum of American Jewish History*. $65.

Estrog box. Brass. M. Shalem. Israel. *in the spirit gallery*. $625.

Left: Estrog box. Hand painted olivewood. 1970s. Israel. Jerusalem cityscape. A view from the Dung Gate leading into the Jewish section. *Alexander Goldfarb collection*. $100.

Below: Side view showing Jerusalem panorama.

Estrog box. Wood/brass plaque with the word "estrog." *in the spirit gallery*. $145.

פרי עץ הדר

Estrog box. Wood/painted enamel. The estrog is a yellow citrus fruit with a lovely smell and a nice taste. *Congregation Keneseth Israel*. $50.

Mizpah. A prayer plaque that is hung on the wall of a home facing east to the Temple mount in Jerusalem. Hand painted. 1880s. *Private collection.*

A mizpah or a menorah. Painted Wood. Paper. Sidi. Israeli. *Edythe Siegel Gallery of American-Jewish Folk Art.* This hanging is hung on the eastern wall of a home as a reminder of the Western Wall in Jerusalem. It can also be used symbolically as a menorah at Hanukkah.

Mizpah. Painted wood and paper. Paper. Sidi. Israeli. *Edythe Siegel Gallery of American-Jewish Folk Art.*

Ushpizen. "To welcome the guests on Succoth." Hand painted wood. S. Kagan/ I.Puski. This prayer shield is hung in the sukkah on one of the three walls. *in the spirit gallery.*

Chapter 7. Hanukkah

Menorahs and Dreidels

It is hard for people who are not Jewish to understand that Hanukkah is not the Jews' Christmas. True, the two holidays share some similarities, the time of year, the gifts, the lighting of lights, a special feast and the presence of a miracle; but while Christmas is a seasonal state of mind involving weeks of anticipation and effort, for many Jews Hanukkah has become just an excuse to have a party for the children. Sadly, many Jews don't even celebrate the holiday once their children have left home. They experience a waiting period until they resume the festivities with their grandchildren.

In fact, Hanukkah recalls an historic military victory in 169-165 B.C.E. and Jews celebrate by giving gifts, sing-

A carving from the Arch of Titus in Rome showing the candelabrum after the destruction of the Temple in 70 A.D. being carried back to Rome in a victory procession.

ing songs, eating latkes, the traditional Hanukkah food of potato pancakes, playing games with a dreidel, a special top, and most important, lighting the Hanukkah lamp or menorah, a candle holder that holds eight lights and also the ninth, the "shamus," the worker, which is used to light the rest.

As a child my favorite part of Hanukkah was the ritual of lighting the Hanukkah lights. Each night with joyous anticipation, I would light the candles, say a blessing and then watch the flickering lights, sparkle, glow and then dissolve into a glob of melted wax.

I have been lighting my own menorah since I was five years old when I was given a small brass menorah with candle holders the size of birthday candles and a lion of Judah engraved on its side. Even then I knew that the Lion of Judah was Judah Maccabee, my role model for Jewish heroes.

As a child, I didn't know many activist Jewish heroes. Unlike Abraham, Moses and Jacob, Judah Maccabee was the stuff of a Saturday matinee movie. After all didn't this brave Jew hide out in caves for years, fight a determined, and at times, hopeless battle against Antiochus, the king of the Syrian-Greeks? Wasn't Judah Maccabee a man who against almost impossible odds, defeated one of the best armies in the world, one even armed with Roman war elephants? And didn't he save the Jewish people, regain control of the holy Temple in Jerusalem and rekindle the Eternal Light with the help of God's miracle of one drop of oil?

Hanukkah remains the holiday of the miracle of the oil. After cleansing the Temple Judah Maccabee found only enough oil to light the Holy Light in the Temple for one night. Miraculously that tiny drop of oil lasted for eight days.

The lesson of Hanukkah has always been that an individual can make a difference. Even the Roman army couldn't stop this determined, morally indignant man and his brothers, from saving not only the Temple, but the rights of the Jewish people to practice their religion.

Years later, in the 1950s in Sunday school, I would be taught that Judah Maccabee was like a Jewish George Washington, fighting the first battle for self determination and democracy, but I preferred my own interpretation. God sends heroes along in times of trouble to remind us that we can help ourselves.

And in the early twentieth century, Theodore Herzl, the founder of the modern Zionist movement proclaimed, "I believe that a wondrous generation of Jews will spring into existence, the Maccabees will rise again."

The Hebrew word *Hanukkah* means "dedication" and Hanukkah, which is called both the Festival of Lights and the Feast of Dedication, is celebrated on the twenty-fifth day of Kislev, the day that the Maccabees cleansed and rededicated the Temple.

Today Jewish families recite the following prayers:

"Baruch atah Adonai eloheinu melech ha olum asher kid'shanu b'mitz va tov v'tzi vanu l'had lik ner shel Hanukkah."

"Blessed art thou O Lord our God, king of the universe who has commanded us to light the Hanukkah lights."

"Baruch atah Adonai eloheinu melech ha olum sh'asa nissim lavoteynu bayamin haham bazman hazeh.".

"Blessed art Thou O Lord our God, king of the universe who performed miracles for our ancestors."

And on the first night only,

"Baruch atah Adonai eloheinu melech ha olum shehiyanu vikimanu vihianu lazman hazeh."

"Blessed art Thou O Lord our God, king of the universe, who has kept us alive and sustained us and brought us to this moment."

Masada was the site of the summer palace of King Herod and the site of a fight for freedom against the Roman armies. In 73 A.D., a band of 960 Jewish zealots fought for three years against the Romans. When defeat was inevitable, the Israelis made a suicide pact and killed each other rather than being taken captive by the Romans. Since then, the Israeli army has taken as its motto, "Masada shall not fall again."

A view from the top of Masada looking out on the Judean desert and the Roman camps below.

The signatures show two distinct characters. One of their contemporaries commented that "they were big women who wore big hats and held strong opinions."

Hanukkah Plate. Redware covered with a white slip. Celia and Alice Silverberg. USA. 1930s. The plate says "Not by power. Not by might. Not by spirit alone." Celia Silverberg (1893-1979) and her sister Alice (1896-1976) lived in Buffalo, New York and were highly educated and deeply religious women who observed the Jewish dietary laws. The two sisters held doctorates in psychology and home economics but lived reclusive lives. They installed a kiln in their bedroom and created Judaica. *Rabbi Abraham Feldman Museum of the Congregation of Beth Israel.* $6000.

Menorah or Mizpah. Hand-painted wood and paper. Sidi. Israeli. 20th century. Notice how the artist incorporated the shapes of two of the Hanukkah symbols, the menorah and the dreidel. *Edythe Siegel Gallery of American-Jewish Folk Art.*

Beginning in December, boxes of Hanukkah candles begin to appear in supermarkets and synagogue gift shops all over the world.

Hanukkah Plate. Hand-painted tin. Artist unknown.
in the spirit gallery. $150.

Hanukkah is one of the best known of the Jewish holidays because it falls at the same time as the Christians celebrate Christmas. The Torah tells the Jews that God is everywhere. This kitchen magnet is just another expression of belief in God and Jewish holidays.

The menorah and the dreidel are important parts of the celebration and retelling of the Hanukkah story. They are also the two best known articles of Judaica. A menorah can assume any shape and be designed like a traditional tree branched candelabra, or the Eastern European styled bench menorah, or a 20th century abstraction. But all menorahs must have eight candle holders and a shammus. Dreidels are spinning tops and must have the four Hebrew letters- "shin," "nun," "gimmel" and "het" on each of its four sides.

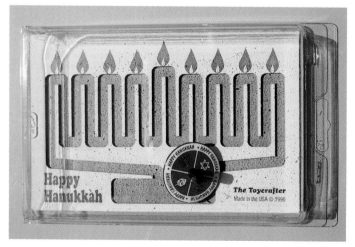

Hanukkah game with a dreidel. Toycrafter. Hanukkah is a time for games and celebrations. $8.

104

Menorahs

The most visible and well known symbol of the Jewish religion is the Hanukkah lamp or candelabra, the *menorah*. Originally God ordered that the Jews make a seven-branched candelabra while in the desert (Exodus 25: 31-40) and thus the first menorahs used by the Jews in the Temple in Jerusalem were seven-branched, but after the destruction of the Temple in 70 B.C.E., it was forbidden to reproduce images from the Temple including the seven-branched menorah. Later during the Middle Ages, an eight-branched menorah was introduced for Hanukkah use.

The image of the menorah has been used for thousands of years by both Jewish and non-Jewish artists and artisans. One of the best known images of the seven branched menorah can be found on the Arch of Titus in Rome. It was Titus, who in the first century B.C.E. destroyed the second Temple and carried its candelabra back to Rome in a triumphal procession.

But actually the first Hanukkah lamps were probably more like the simple clay oil lamps in use during the Roman era. And in early Hanukkah practices these lamps were lined up each night of Hanukkah and filled with oil.

Today while Hanukkah menorahs are eight-branched with an extra arm for the shammus, the seven branched menorah is still the official emblem of the state of Israel.

While early menorahs were tree-branched candelabras, during the 17th, 18th and 19th centuries, menorahs began to assume different styles and soon menorahs were free-standing, hung on the wall or were placed on a shelf.

"It is a religious precept to place the Hanukkah lamp by the door which is near the public domain, in such a manner that the mezuzah should be on the right hand and the Hanukkah lamp is on the left."

It has been suggested that bench and shelf menorahs came about by necessity. Some Jewish scholars have suggested that the Hanukkah lamp was first placed inside the house so that Jewish families need not flaunt their Jewishness and thus invite persecution. The 'bench" menorah that sat on a shelf or inside a window sill, became popular among Ashkenazi Jews.

Soon menorahs became metaphors for the destroyed Temple in Jerusalem, and as such, artists incorporated architectural motifs in their designs. Soon German and Italian menorahs assumed the look of miniature synagogues and historic buildings of the Diaspora and their decorative elements included columns, pillars, and stairs. There are many examples of menorahs which resemble 16th century Italian High Baroque temples, Moorish filigree palaces and 19th century neo-classical German buildings.

During the 15th century and the days of Spanish Inquisition, the Marranos or the Spanish Jews who worshipped in secret, created new kinds of menorahs. These

Eternal light lamp. Judah Maccabee re-lit the Eternal Light after he rescued and cleansed the desecrated Temple in Jerusalem. Instead of lasting for one night, the oil burned for eight days and became known as the miracle of Hanukkah. Today the Jews celebrate this miracle by lighting the menorah for eight days. *Congregation Keneseth Israel.* $1000.

A Hellenistic oil lamp B.C.E. 50. Probably lamps similar to this were used in biblical times to celebrate Judah Maccabee's miracle.

Marrano-styled menorahs were usually small chests concealing spaces inside for eight candles or oil wicks.

But while menorahs may change its shape and reflect the different influences of the many cultures to which the Jewish people were exposed, the function has never changed. All menorahs hold the eight lights of Hanukkah.

It is assumed that the order of lighting the Hanukkah candles is a cumulative act, and each night, one more candle is lit until the eighth night. But in fact this has not always been the case. In the second century, there was a disagreement among the rabbis about the order and the rabbinic schools of Hillel and Shammai debated whether or not one should light the candles one by one or light all eight the first night and then decrease the number, leaving only one candle on the last night.

The dispute was finally settled by Rabbi Hillel who decreed that the Hanukkah lights should be increased each night since the holiness of the holiday should increase and not decrease.

For centuries Jews have followed the rabbinical injunction that the Hanukkah lights must be placed in a single row. But in the twentieth century, many modern artists have improvised in the placement of the candles and have created irregular patterns.

Today menorahs are the most commonly collected Judaica. Many families own at least two menorahs so that each member can light his or her own. Today there are post-modernist menorahs, neo-classical menorahs, menorahs celebrating American patriotism, menorahs made from glass, brass, silver and gold. Mexican-made menorahs are as gaudy and colorful as Mexican pinatas. Israeli menorahs often resemble the traditional stone structures of Jerusalem.

Menorahs have either candle holders or containers, often a small pitcher for an oil wick. But all are part of the celebration of the miracle of the Hanukkah oil.

Menorah. Brass. Eilat stone. Israel. 1980s. The first menorahs were in the traditional shape of a tree-branched candelabra similar to those used in the Temple of Solomon in Jerusalem. This menorah, which was made in the 1980s, has an Eilat stone in the center. These blue and turquoise stones are commonly found in the sea-side resort of Eilat which is on the Red Sea, overlooking the Jordanian city of Aquaba. *Collection of Laurence Goldfarb.* $80.

Menorah. Brass. 1980s. Israel. This menorah is marked Israel in both English and Hebrew. $80.

Candelabra. Silver. 1800s. Many pieces are considered Judaica, only through use and tradition. This candelabra was given to Congregation Beth Israel by a congregant. Some have said that while it is traditional to have an eight branched Hanukkah lamp, sometimes Jews had to conceal their religion and used generic items to observe in secret. *Rabbi Abraham Feldman Museum of the Congregation Beth Israel.*

Candelabra. Brass. A seven-branched candelabra used in Sabbath services. In Exodus the Lord commands the Israelites to make a candlestick with three branches on one side and three branches on the other. This is the origin of the seven-armed candle holder found in synagogues and temples since biblical times. *Rabbi Abraham Feldman Museum of the Congregation Beth Israel.*

Menorah. Brass. Bench-type. Russian. 1900s. Note the traditional Hanukkah symbols. Judah Maccabee was called the Lion of Judah. *Estate of Mrs. Mayer Yellin.*

Menorah. Cast iron. 1970s. Israel. Candleholders can either hold candles or be filled with oil and lit with wicks. The small pitcher, the shammus, can be filled with oil or hold a candle. *Mrs. Lillian Altman Collection.*

Menorah/Sabbath Candlesticks. 19th century Polish/cast iron. Often Polish Jews would add Sabbath light holders to the menorah so that when the Sabbath came during Hanukkah all the candles would be lit in the same candle holder.

Menorah. Repousse silver 19th century Hanukkah lamp from Eastern Europe. This menorah has many typical Hanukkah symbols. The Ten Commandments show the law. The lions of Judah refer to Judah Maccabee. The jugs, which can either be used as holder for oil wicks or small candles, refer to the miracle of light. *Congregation Keneseth Israel.* $1000.

Menorah. Brass. A 20th century copy of a bench-style menorah popular in eastern Europe. *National Museum of American Jewish History.* $295.

Menorah. Brass based on an early Italian design. L. Meiselman. *in the spirit gallery.* $325

Menorah. Pewter. German/Dutch. 1750. The two hanging buckets are intended to carry the oil to light the menorah. This was an early hanging type Hanukkah lamp. The two holes in the center were placed there to attach the lamp to a wall. *Rabbi Abraham Feldman Museum of the Congregation Beth Israel.*

Menorah. Silver. *The National Museum of American Jewish History.*

Menorah. Silver. 1850. German. The shamus stands off to the side and on the left is a jug to hold the oil. Most early menorahs were oil lamps. *Rabbi Abraham Feldman Museum of the Congregation Beth Israel.*

Menorah. Brass. 18th century. Italian. This menorah has a very classical design and is unusual in that it has a very plain back splash. Usually menorahs are more ornate. *Private collection.*

Menorah. Silver. 19th century.

Menorah. Brass repousse. 17th century. *Rabbi Abraham Feldman Museum of the Congregation Beth Israel.*

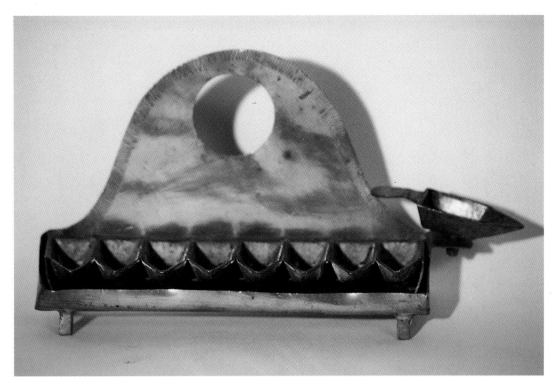

Menorah. Pewter. German/Dutch 19th century miniature pewter hanging lamp. Pewter was commonly used by the Jews in the 18th and 19th centuries since it was a cheaper metal than brass or silver. *Rabbi Abraham Feldman Museum of the Congregation Beth Israel.*

Menorah. Pewter.Safat. Israel. 20th century. *Private collection.*

Menorah. Brass. Footed Hanukkah lamp. German. 1800. Note the two holders for the Shabbat. *Rabbi Abraham Feldman Museum of the Congregation Beth Israel.*

Menorah. Silver filigree. Baal Shem Tov menorah. Poland. 18th or 19th century. It was said that the 18th century Hasidic master, the Baal Shem Tov, used this type of menorah in Poland. From then on it was widely copied in the Ukraine and in Poland. *Private collection.*

Menorah. Brass. Ivriah menorah. *Private collection.*

Menorah. Brass. 1920s. Ivriah was a group of Jewish women living in New York in the 1920s who tried to set up classes to learn Hebrew. *Private collection.*

Menorah. 1950 cast bronze in the shape of an Israeli soldier. Israel. *Private collection.*

Menorah, Green patina metal. Judah Maccabee. 1950s. Pal-bel. Israel. *Private collection.*

Menorah. Brass. Green metal. Pal-bel. Israel. 1950s. *Private collection.*

Menorah. Silver. 20th century. *The National Museum of American Jewish History.* $150.

Menorah. Tin. A 1960s Barton candy give-away. *Private collection.*

Menorah. Brass. 20th century. Reproduction of a Wolpert designed menorah. *The National Museum of American Jewish History*. $250.

Menorah. A 20th century copy of a Wolpert design. *Congregation Keneseth Israel*. $80.

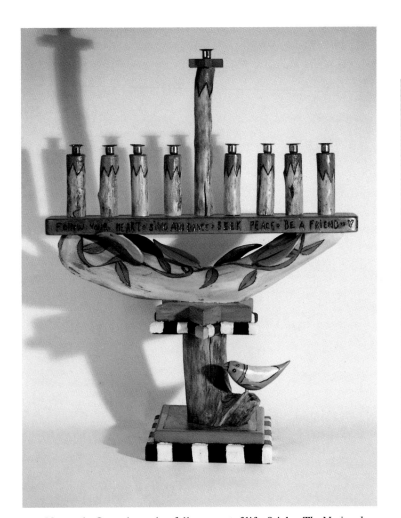

Menorah. Carved wooden folk art tree of life. Sticks. *The National Museum of American Jewish History*. $450.

Menorah. Brass. *National Museum of American Jewish History*.

Menorah. Hand blown Glass. Limited edition floating glass menorah. 1994. Ray King. USA. *The National Museum of American Jewish History*. $2400.

Menorah. Standing Hanukkah candelabra. Sheffield silver. England. 1800. Many wealthy Jews would buy pieces from some of the leading silversmiths of the day. This candelabra shows a grace that is not found in later Eastern European menorahs. *Rabbi Abraham Feldman Museum of the Congregation Beth Israel.*

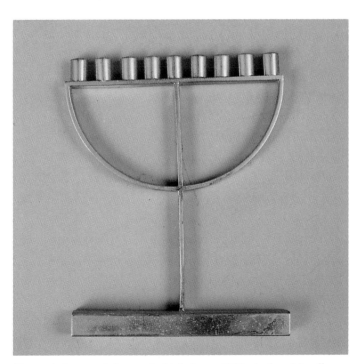

Menorah. brass. miniature. L. Meiselman. USA. *in the spirit gallery*. $95.

Menorah. Glass. Artist unknown. *in the spirit gallery*. $175.

Menorah. Brass. Manfred Anson. The Liberty Bell Menorah. 1980s. *Private collection.*

Menorah. Statue of Liberty menorah commissioned by Mark and Peachy Levy for the Skirball Museum. The statues refer to the Jewish experience— Israel, the Galut, and the Holocaust. *Private collection.*

Above: Menorah. Brass circa 1948. *Estate of B.W. Green.* $1500.

Left: Menorah. Ceramic. Garson/Pakele. *in the spirit gallery.* $450.

Menorah. Amy's ark. Aluminum. *in the spirit gallery.* $350.

Menorah. Gold over bronze. Judith Brown. *in the spirit gallery.* $3200.

Menorah. Ceramic. Judy Dalombo. *in the spirit gallery.* $150.

Menorah and dreidel. Wood. *The National Museum of American Jewish History.* $100.

117

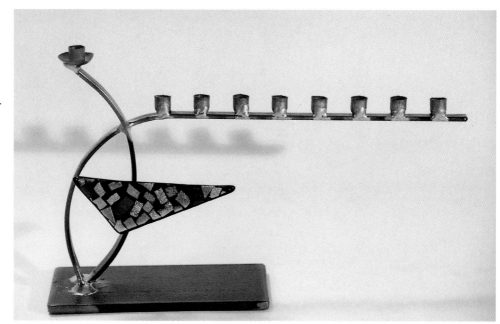

Menorah. Glass/enamel. Gary Rosenthal.
USA. *The National Museum of American
Jewish History.* $90.

Menorah. Bronze. Dancers' menorah
based on a design by David Klass. *The
National Museum of American Jewish
History.* $150.

Menorah. Aluminum. Markussen.
*The National Museum of American
Jewish History.* $150.

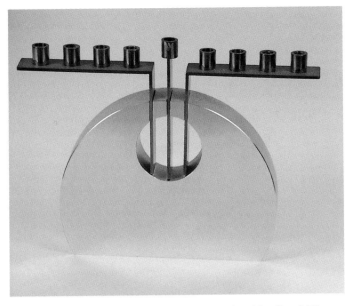

Menorah. Brass/aluminum. R. Landau. Israel. *in the spirit gallery.* $425

Menorah. Steel. Jewish Museum collection. Larry Kagan. Kagan was a student of Moshe Zabari at the Tobe-Pascher School of the Jewish Museum. Kagan made this menorah out of an old street grate. *in the spirit gallery.* $3000.

Menorah. Sterling/bronze. Hana Geber. *in the spirit gallery.* $10,000.

Above: Menorah. Glass. Keleman. *The National Museum of American Jewish History.* $550.

Right: Menorah. Stained glass/ copy of a fragment from an illustration from an Italian tapestry circa 1700 showing the Temple Mount, Moses with the Ten Commandments, and his brother Aaron. Leona Fein. *The National Museum of American Jewish History.* $200.

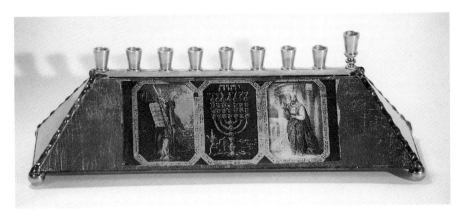

Menorah. brass. M.Shalem. *in the spirit gallery*. $65.

Menorah. Aluminum/brass. S. Freiman. Israel. *in the spirit gallery*. $1200.

Menorah. Enamel/wrought iron. K. Rossi. *in the spirit gallery*. $395.

Menorah. Stained glass/ fragment from a Damascus, Syria 1883 Ketubah. Leona Fein. *in the spirit gallery*. $250.

Menorah. Pottery/enamel. Miera Una. Israel. *in the spirit gallery*. $1200.

enorah. Silverplate. Mass produced bench-type grape arbor sign. *The National Museum of American Jewish History*. $85.

Menorah. Ceramic. Shlomit. Israel. Notice the raised circle for the shammus. *in the spirit gallery*. $295.

Menorah. Ceramic. Richard McBee. USA. Moses receiving the Ten Commandments. *in the spirit gallery*. $1800.

Menorah. Contemporary ceramic. Gaia Smith. "Cityscape." *The National Museum of American Jewish History.* $550.

Menorah. The synagogues of Jerusalem. Rear view. *Museum of Modern Art.* $100.

Menorah. Ceramic. A reconstruction of Jerusalem showing the Mosque of Omar behind the surviving western wall of Solomon's Temple. In the foreground are two of the Jewish synagogues. *The National Museum of American Jewish History.* $190.

Menorah. Brass/plexiglass. Dalia. *in the spirit gallery.* $325.

Menorah. Anodized aluminum star-shaped menorah. Peter Handler. *The National Museum of American Jewish History.* $165.

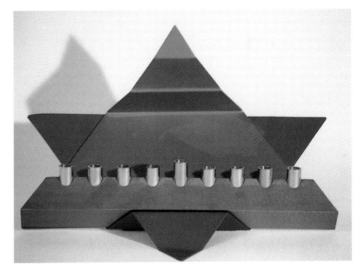

Menorah. Ceramic. B. Lenore. USA. *in the spirit gallery.* $295.

123

Menorah. Ceramic. Linda Relin. *The National Museum of American Jewish History.* $350.

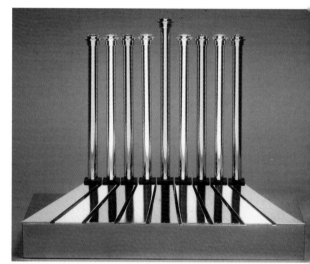

Menorah. *in the spirit gallery.*

Menorah, dreidel and tzedakah box. *in the spirit gallery.*

Menorah. Brass. Miniature. This menorah was given to the author when she was five years old. 1950s. USA.

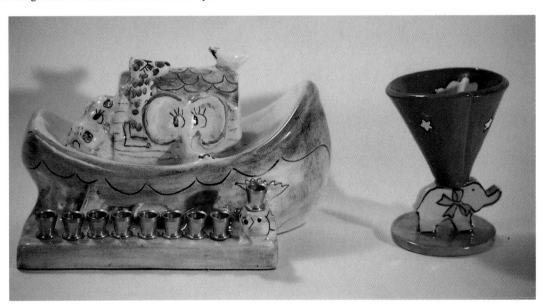

Menorah. Ceramic. Children's Noah ark. Baby's cup, Myra Kaplan. *The National Museum of American Jewish History.* menorah$95, cup $50.

Menorah. Fire engine. $95.

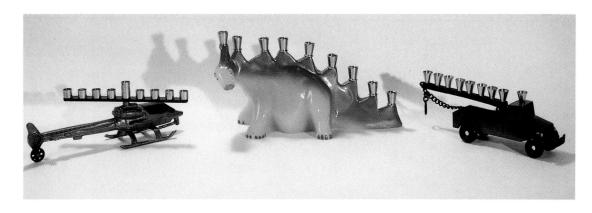

Menorahs. *The National Museum of American Jewish History*. Helicopter $36. Dinosaur $48. Tow truck. $36.

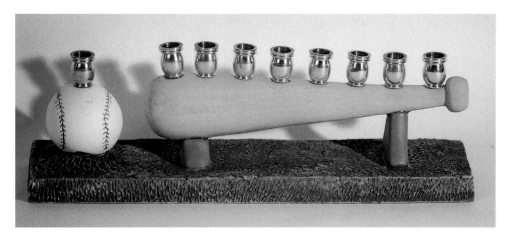

Menorah. Painted wood. *National Museum of American Jewish History*. $50.

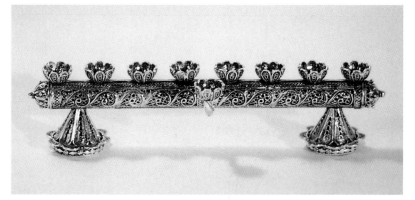

Menorah. Silver filigree. *National Museum of American Jewish History*. $496.

Above: Menorah. Silver. miniature. travel. *The National Museum of American Jewish History*. $80.

Right: Menorahs. Traveling menorahs. Left: cast aluminum with prayer on the lid. Right: brass A. Solomon. Israel. Marrano Jews had to worship in secret so often they hid their religious objects, concealing them in chests or in objects that seemed to have other functions. *in the spirit gallery*. $130.

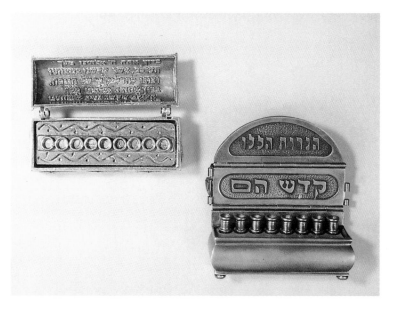

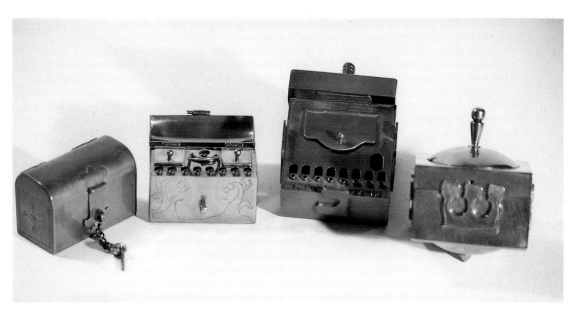

Menorahs. Two traveling menorahs. One is concealed in a chest. The other is a dreidel/menorah. Brass. M. Shalem. *Brenda Bernstein collection.*

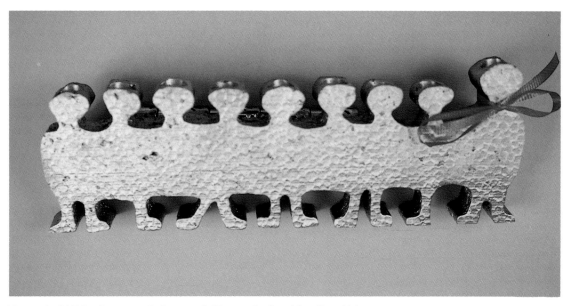

Menorah. Children's menorah. Pewter. S. Kagan. *in the spirit gallery.* $95.

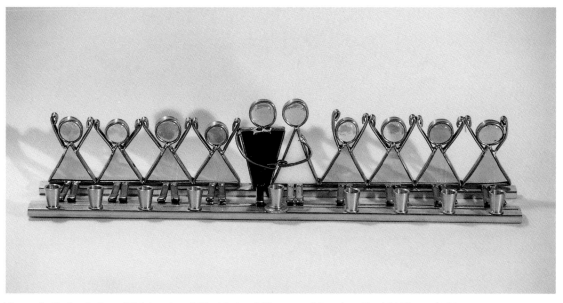

Menorah. Stained glass. "Celebration." *The National Museum of American Jewish History.* $130.

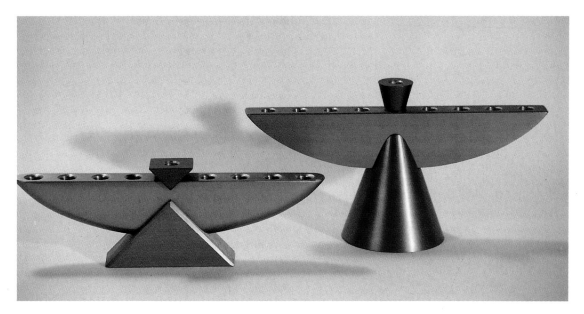

Menorahs. Anodized aluminum. Peter Handler. *The National Museum of American Jewish History*. $195.

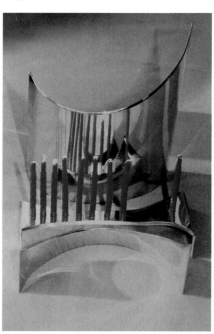

Menorah. "Triumph Triumvirate." 1989. Judith E. Goldstein. Three pieces of pewter. This menorah sculpture is created in three parts to show that the Jewish people must stand alone against oppressors as did Judah Maccabee and together as a people as they have through the ages. *Photography by Judith E. Goldstein*. $700.

Menorah. Blue and white jewel tone glass. *The National Museum of American Jewish History*. $165.

Menorah. Dove Menorah. Peter Shire. *Audrey's at the Skirball Cultural Center and Museum.* $500

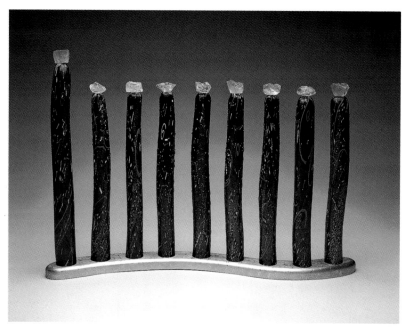

Menorah. Colored glass. *Kerry Feldman*

Menorah. Painted brass. 1960s. *Estate of Sophie R. Yellin.*

Dreidels

"Dreidel, dreidel, dreidel, I made you out of clay and when you are dry and ready, then dreidel I will play." "*Sevivon, sov, sov, sov.*" (Dreidel, turn, turn, turn.)

The dreidel, which comes from the German word to spin, is another Hanukkah symbol. In the days of Antiochus, the Jews were not allowed to practice their religion so they would study the Torah secretly. They would place a dreidel on a nearby table and when the soldiers approached they would spin the top as a subterfuge. Since the four sided top has Hebrew letters on each side.."nun, gimmel, het and shin," the Rabbis devised a game out of these letters, which stood for the phrase, "A great miracle happened 'here'." (Israelis substitute the word "shin" (there) for a "pay" which stands for "po," (here) meaning "a great miracle happened `here.'" Playing with the dreidel became a means of affirming a relationship with God.

Eighteenth and nineteenth century dreidels were made of wood, ivory, or lead. In eastern Europe dreidels were usually made out of lead. Twentieth century dreidels have been made from wood, plastic, and glass.

Dreidels are typically part of the Hanukkah celebrations and dreidel favors filled with Hanukkah gelt are some of the more modern innovations. The game is played by betting a token and then spinning the top. If the dreidel lands on "nun," the spinner gets nothing. If gimmel, the spinner gets the entire pot. If "het," half and "shin" means that the spinner must put a token into the pot.

Dreidels. Silver. *The National Museum of American Jewish History.* $35-200.

Dreidels. Wood. Toycrafter makes eight different styles of dreidels. $

Dreidel. Wood. Toycrafter. $3.

Dreidels are spinning tops used on Hanukkah. These four-sided tops contain the four Hebrew letters "nun," "gimmel," "shin" and "het." These words are an anagram for "a great miracle happened there." In Israel "pay" is substituted for "shin" meaning "a great miracle happened here." When the game is played, if the dreidel falls on "nun," the spinner gets nothing. If it falls on "het," the spinner gets half; "gimmel," the spinner gets everything; and "shin," the spinner must give to the pot.

Dreidels. Silver. Pewter. *in the spirit gallery*. $110.

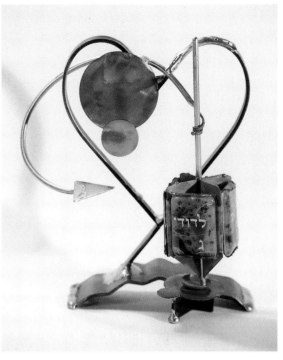

Dreidel. Stained glass/metal. Gary Rosenthal. U.S.A. *The National Museum of American Jewish History*. $130.

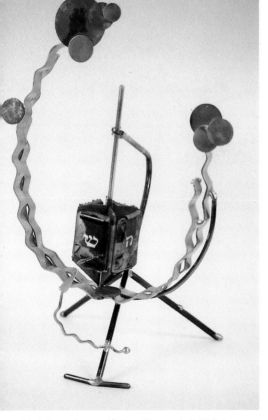

Dreidel. Brass/enamel. Gary Rosenthal. U.S.A. *in the spirit gallery*. $185.

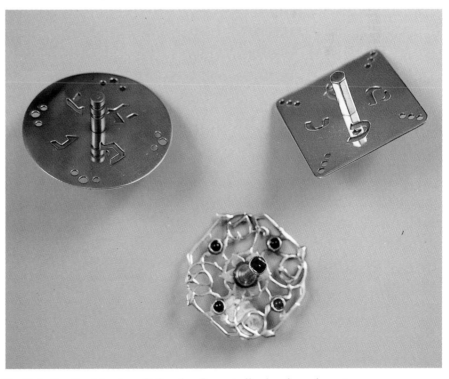

Dreidels. Sterling/titanium. R. Landau. Lace sterling/semi-precious stones. *in the spirit gallery*. Titan. $110. Lace $95.

Dreidel. Hand-painted wood. Crystal. *Congregation Keneseth Israel.* $10-50.

Dreidel. Ceramic. C. Brull. *in the spirit gallery*. $195.

Dreidel. "Rhythms of Note." 1990 Judith E. Goldstein. Pewter with an ebony violin tuning peg and a sterling silver charm. The Hebrew letters alternate with rhythmic musical notes. *Photography by Judith E. Goldstein*. $135.

Dreidel. Hand painted wood. Artist: Sarah. USA. *in the spirit gallery*. $18.

Dreidel. *in the spirit gallery.*

Dreidel. *in the spirit gallery.*

Dreidel. *In the spirit gallery.*

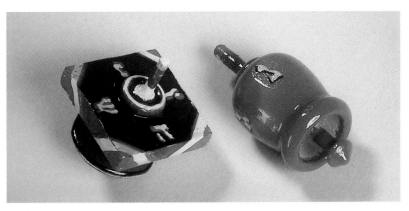

Dreidel. *The National Museum of American Jewish History.*

Dreidel. *The National Museum of American Jewish History.*

133

Chaper 8. Purim

Megillahs and Groggers

It's been a long time since I made myself a yellow paper crown and dressed up like Queen Esther for Purim, but I think of Queen Esther each year as I notice boxes of Hamantaschen, pastries in the shape of a three cornered hat, arrive on the bakery shelves.

The story of Purim is a simple one. It is one of the few holidays in the Jewish religion where the hero is a woman and a young and pretty one at that. Esther was picked out of thousands of young women to become the second wife of the king of Persia, Ahasuerus. Cautioned by her uncle Mordechai, she concealed the fact that she was a Jew, and followed his instructions to become a good wife.

The story could have ended there, but it didn't. When Esther learned that her husband's trusted advisor, Haman, was plotting to kill all the Jews in Shusan, she devised a plan at a great risk to herself to expose him, save the Jews, and still keep her husband's love.

I still remember my childish glee and triumph when dressed like what I thought was a 5th century Persian queen, I looked forward to scream, yell and whirl my grogger or noisemaker to drown out Haman's name every time it was mentioned in the reading of the megillah, the Purim story.

For many young Jewish girls, it would be the example of Queen Esther that would inspire them to tackle unpopular causes, fight prejudice and hypocrisy, and not be afraid to put themselves on the line. Esther has become a role model who has survived history. To me it is interesting that even the ancient rabbis who did not allow women to participate in the hierarchy of the Jewish religion were impressed by Esther's initiative. In fact they instructed men to read the Purim story once, and then drink and rejoice, and women to read the story twice.

Purim occurs during the Hebrew month of Adar. The word *Purim* means the casting of lots and in fact the story of Purim centers around the gamble taken by a young Jewish woman named Esther and it is her story that is read during the Purim service.

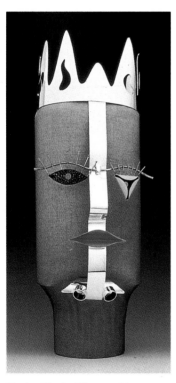

Purim Mask. Silver, gold, enamel; fabricated, pierced, and formed. Moshe Zabari (b. 1935). 1992. This mask has references to the four characters in the Book of Esther— the crown of the king Ahasuerus; an eye in the shape of a hamantashen, the traditional sweet for purim in the shape of Haman's hat; the eyes and lips of Queen Esther; and the nostrils of Mordechai's horse. *Collection of the artist. Photography by D.R. Guthrie.*

In this folk art painting by the Israeli artist Sidi, Haman drives Mordechai who holds his grogger in his hand. The Hebrew letters say Mordechai and Haman. *Edythe Siegel Gallery of American-Jewish Folk Art.*

134

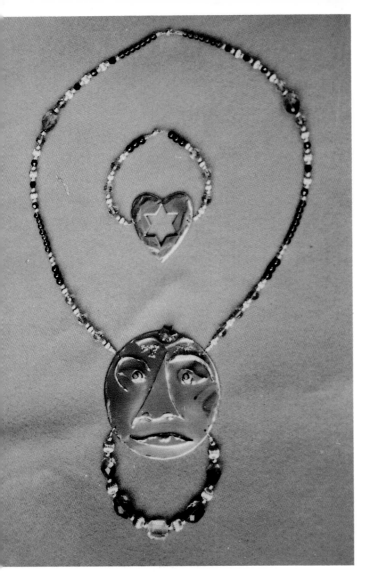

Purim Plate. Redware covered with a white slip. circa 1930s. Celia and Alice Silverberg. *Rabbi Abraham Feldman Museum of the Congregation Beth Israel.*

"The Purim Players" Queen Esther. Pewter with beads of amethyst, garnet, Swarovski Austrian crystal, silver and gold. 1988. The Queen is dressed in royal purple amethysts and vibrant garnets. The hidden cut-out of the Star of David in the bracelet shows that the Queen must hide her Jewishness. The inspiration for this design was that of the artist's mother-in-law, Esther. *Judith E. Goldstein. Photography by Judith E. Goldstein.* $450.

Megillah

The Megillah, the story of Esther, unlike the Torah is wound around one scroll, and is read only during the holiday of Purim. And like the Torah, the megillah is written entirely by hand with a reed or a goose quill.

Ever since the Middle Ages Jewish sages have ornamented the Megillah with beautiful illustrations and ornate calligraphy. Special Megillah cases were carved out of wood, silver and gold. One of the earliest known Megillahs was dated 1637.

The Megillah is read twice during the Purim service. But because the Talmud says that Purim was a miracle where God worked mysteriously, His name does not appear at all in the Megillah text. And because of His mysterious presence, Jews dress up in costumes and assume Purim masquerades.

Megillah. Silver. Late 19th- to early 20th-century. *Rabbi Abraham Feldman Museum of the Congregation Beth Israel.*

135

Megillah case. Wood. *Congregation Keneseth Israel.*

Megillah. Ivory. Parchment. Antique circa 1800s. *Congregation Keneseth Israel.* $1000.

Megillah. Silver miniature Persian megillah with jewels. Late 17th century. *Congregation Keneseth Israel.* $1000.

Megillah. Olivewood. 18th century Persia. *Rabbi Abraham Feldman Museum of the Congregation Beth Israel.*

Megillah. Silver. Parchment.
Illuminated Megillah.
Morocco. Late 19th century.
Congregation Keneseth Israel.
$2000.

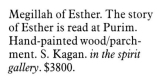

Casting lots at Purim.

Megillah of Esther. The story
of Esther is read at Purim.
Hand-painted wood/parch-
ment. S. Kagan. *in the spirit
gallery*. $3800.

Megillah. Silver. 20th century. *Private collection.*

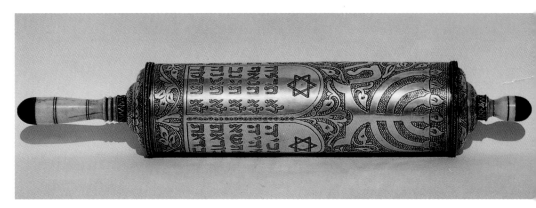

Detail

Purim Plate. Silver. Hana Geber. *Nancy Berman and Alan Bloch Collection.*

Megillah cases. Silver, wood. M. Singer. *in the spirit gallery*. $375. and $295.

Grogger

The custom of using the grogger, the noisemaker used in Purim celebrations, began in thirteenth century France and Germany. Every time Haman's name is mentioned in the reading of the Megillah, the grogger is swung around and around with vigor and joy to drown out Haman's name. Today groggers are made of wood, silver, lead, pewter, ceramic and plastic.

Originally groggers were adaptations of the noisemakers and devices to frighten away evil spirits. The Jews took this custom and adapted it to the story of Esther and Haman. Booing the villain has been popular with audiences since the 18th century. During the 19th and twentieth centuries, melodramas became a popular theatrical entertainment, and booing and hissing the villain became a part of the expected audience reaction.

Ushpizen are another part of the Purim service. It is symbolic to invite special guests from the Bible on each night of the holiday and talk about their contributions to Jewish history. It is also customary to send out food to friends and gifts to the poor on special Purim plates. In some communities it is the custom to hold a Purim Masquerade Charity Ball as part of the holiday celebrations.

During the celebration of Purim, the story of Esther is read during the service. The book of Esther is called the Megillah. Children usually dress up like the Purim characters. During the service when Haman's name is read, children use groggers or noisemakers to drown out his name. Groggers can be made of wood, metals, or plastic.

Right: Grogger. Silver/brass. Polish. Circa 1920s. There is the Hebrew inscription, "cursed Haman." *Rabbi Abraham Feldman Museum of the Congregation Beth Israel.*

Grogger. Wood. German. Late 19th century. The carver of this grogger was obviously a cabinet or furniture maker. Groggers are adaptations of noisemakers and devices to frighten evil spirits. The Jews took this custom and adapted it to the story of Esther and Haman. Jews use groggers during the reading of the story of Esther to drown out the name of the evil Haman. Booing the villain became a part of 19th and early 20th century melodramas when the audiences would hiss and boo whenever the villain came on stage. *Congregation Keneseth Israel.* $400.

Grogger. Wood. 20th century.

Above: Grogger. Silver. Bier. Israel. *in the spirit gallery.* $495.

Right: Groggers. Sterling. Bier. Israel. *in the spirit gallery.* $185.

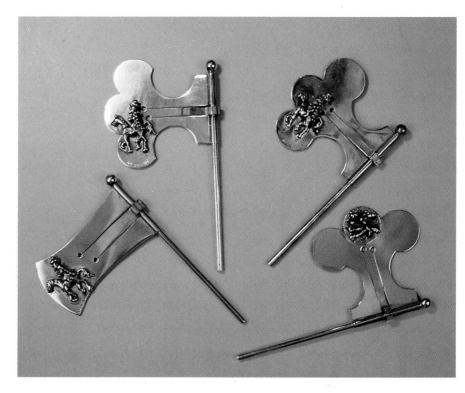

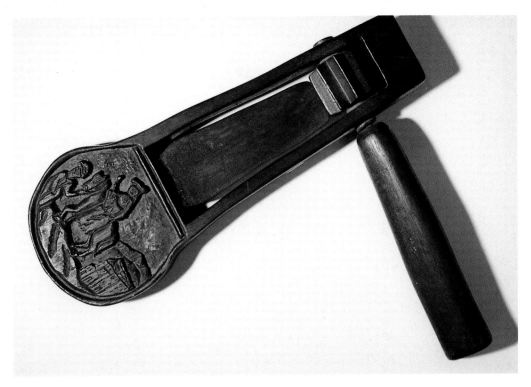

Grogger. Hand-carved wood. Herman Braginsky. USA. *in the spirit gallery*. $1400.

Grogger. Wood. *in the spirit gallery*.

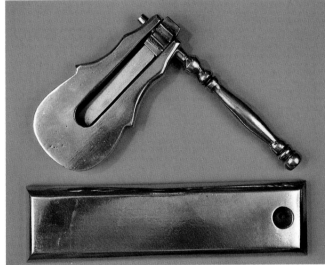

Above: Grogger. Aluminum. M. Singer. USA. *in the spirit gallery*. $195.

Left: Grogger. Brass. M. Shalem. Israel. *in the spirit gallery*. $500.

Grogger. Hand-painted wood. *in the spirit gallery*. $275.

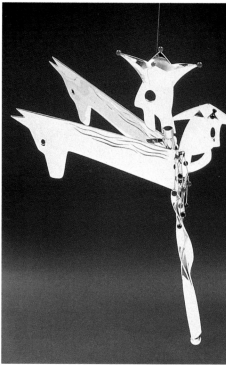

Purim noisemaker (grogger). Silver. Moshe Zabari (b. 1935). 1992. Silver with beads of carnelian, lapis, and green onyx; fabricated, hammered, and pierced, 17 X 9 1/2". Haman is shown seated backward on a horse in the manner often used to depict Jews in anti-semitic caricatures. *Museum purchase with funds provided by Suzanne and Paul Kester, HUC Skirball Cultural Center and Museum(HUCSM), museum collection. Photography by D.R. Guthrie, Jerusalem.*

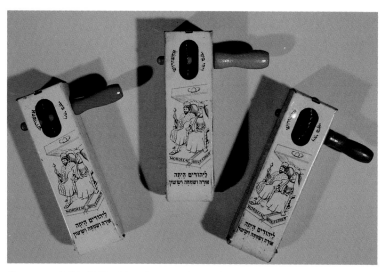

Groggers. 1950-1960s. Tin. Commonly used by American Jewish school children. *Wilbur, Sara, and Paris Pierce Collection.*$100.

Groggers. Wood. Home-made noise makers. USA. Early 1920s. *Wilbur, Sara, and Paris Pierce Collection.*$100.

Chapter 9. Passover

Haggadahs, Seder plates, Elijah's cups, hand washers, matzah covers, Miriam's cup, charoseth plates.

For years my memories of Jewish holiday meals have been filled with the comfort foods of tradition especially at Passover or Pesach-chicken soup, matzah balls, roast chicken, charoseth, and sponge or angel cakes and macaroons. Matzah balls and chicken soup are the glue that have held families together for generations.

Each year, as I gather the Passover haggadahs (prayer books) to set the table, I think a lot about the fact that "seder" means order, and that each year at Passover we conduct ourselves the same way according to tradition.

Seders have helped keep the fabric of Jewish society together for thousands of years. At the seder we talk of service to others and service to God rather than self service. In the center of the table in every Jewish home are the symbols of the Passover story, the flight of the Jews from Egyptian bondage..the lamb shank, the egg, the bitter herbs, the charoseth, the sweet mixture of apples, nuts, cinnamon and wine, the salt water, the green vegetable, the goblet of wine for the prophet Elijah and the three matzah. And each year the head of the family opens the Haggadah and tells the same Passover story, says the same prayers, sings the same songs and serves the same menu.

And each year the youngest child asks the same four questions, beginning with the first question, "Why is this night different from all other nights?' And each year we read about four sons. The one who is wise, the one who is contrary, the one who is simple and the one who does not even know how to ask a question. And each year we read that the worst sin is not knowing how to ask.

But while the seder is a holiday feast, it is also the holiday that recalls that time in history when Moses rescued the Jewish people from Egyptian bondage and led them closer to the Promised Land of Israel.

The matzah, the unleavened bread of the Exodus is one of the most significant symbols of the Passover story as is the Passover story. The matzah is a symbol of the sacrifices people make for freedom, and reminds us that once the Jews were slaves in Egypt. The three matzahs used during the service symbolize the three patriarchs of the bible, Abraham, Isaac, and Jacob. as well as the three groups of the Jewish people Cohen, Levi and Israel.

The text of the Passover service is found in the Haggadah. Haggadah comes from the Hebrew word "to tell." The Haggadah that Jews use today is the legacy of the Ashkenazi Jews of Eastern Europe and it was these Jews who added many of the now traditional songs sung during the seder such as *"Dayenu," "Had Gadya,"* and *"Adir Hu."*

Jewish artists from 14th century Spain, 16th century Holland and 17th and 18th century Germany, have been fascinated by the artistic possibilities of the Haggadah. Among the most famous were 14th century Spanish haggadahs and 16th century Amsterdam Haggadahs. Ben Shahn and Leonard Baskin are just two of the many contemporary American artists who have created beautifully decorated Haggadahs.

Passover seder plates are either divided into sections or bear the names or illustrate the six foods that are associated with the seder -the matzah, the lamb shankbone, the roasted egg, the bitter herbs, the charoseth, and the karpas (the green vegetable). In addition there is a special wine cup for Elijah, a container for salt water and a basin in which to wash the hands as proscribed during the service.

In the 1990s, Jewish feminists added another element to the Passover service and introduced Miriam's cup, to remember Moses' sister Miriam.

The Passover celebration begins at sundown the night before seder when the head of the house conducts a search for any crumbs of leaven bread and using a special candle and a feather, the family conducts a search for leaven which is then burned.

The Judean Desert today, the scene where Moses led the Israelites through the desert.

Seder plate. Pewter. Judith E. Goldstein. USA. "The Waters' Parting." 1994.
The six dishes for the Passover offerings look like waves of water. They also
refer to the tears of the Jewish people when they were slaves in Egypt. *Photography by Judith E. Goldstein.* $1400.

Haggadah. Olivewood. 1893. *Rabbi Abraham Feldman
Museum of the Congregation Beth Israel.*

Haggadah. Olivewood. 1930s. Pre-state of Israel, made
in Jerusalem at the Bezalel School. *Private collection.*

Detail

144

Haggadah. Paper. The Passover Haggadah gives the order of the Passover service. In the 1950s and 1960s haggadahs would be given out free by many food companies such as Maxwell House coffee, Manischevitz etc. This Haggadah was given out by the Jewish Day School in Allentown, PA. to all its students in the 1970s. $10.

Haggadah. Copied and illustrated by Ben Shahn. 1947. *Private collection*. $150.

Detail "One kid, one kid....Chad gad ya."

Haggadah. Drawings by Leonard Baskin. *Estate of Sophie Yellin*. $100.

Illustration by Leonard Baskin of the bitter herbs, "maror," the horseradish root.

Illustration by Leonard Baskin of some of the Ten Plagues.

Seder Plate. Silver. 18th century Germany. In modern times Jewish artists have forsaken the Biblical injunction against creating graven images. *The National Museum of American Jewish History.*

Seder plate. Porcelain. Tepper, London. Circa 1920s. This seder plate has six sections. The additional one is for the salt water. The medallions around the rim give the order of the service. *in the spirit gallery.* $1200.

Backstamp of the Tepper Seder plate.

Seder Plate. Porcelain. Tepper. England. circa 1920s. A Seder plate usually illustrates the Passover story and has five sections for the five foods of the seder service-bitter herbs, charoseth, green vegetable, the shankbone, a roasted egg and a special dish for the matzah and a bowl for the salt water. This plate tells the Passover story. *in the spirit gallery*. $1200.

Another Tepper Plate: c. 1920's. $1200.

Passover Plate. Pewter. 18th century. German. *Rabbi Abraham Feldman Museum of the Congregation Beth Israel.*

Left: Seder Plate. Porcelain. Spode. 1970s. This plate is a modern version of the Tepper plate. It also has six sections and includes a place for the salt water. *Robert Bungerz collection.* $300.

Above: Backstamp of the Spode Seder plate.

The Passover seder table is set with many symbolic ritual items. Seder means the order of service and the seder plate holds the symbolic foods discussed and eaten during the Passover or Pesach service- the bitter herbs, (maror) the charoseth, the green vegetable, (karpas), the roasted shankbone and the roasted egg. In addition there is a bowl for the salt water, a wine glass for the Prophet Elijah and a plate for the three matzah. The prayer book that is read during the seder is called the Haggadah. In the 1990s Jewish feminists have added another element to the seder service, Miriam's cup, to remember Moses' sister, Miriam.

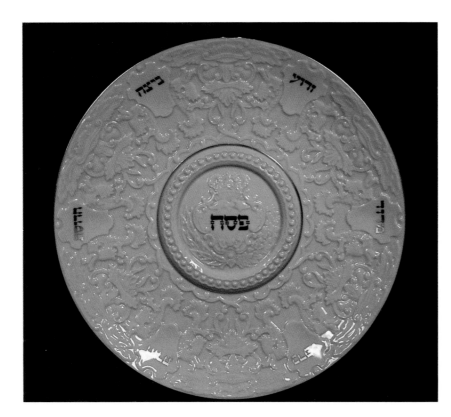

Left: Seder Plate. Lenox china. This plate is an adaptation of a 19th century plate that is now in the collection of the Jewish Museum in New York. 1980s. *Appel's Jewelry Store. Allentown, Pennsylvania.* $120.

Above: Detail

Passover plate. Pewter. 1740. "...And the daughter of Pharoah went down to the river and her maidens walked along the river side and she saw the arc among the reeds and sent her hand maid to fetch it..." Thus begins the Passover story with the discovery of the baby Moses in the bulrushes. *Rabbi Abraham Feldman Museum of the Congregation Beth Israel.*

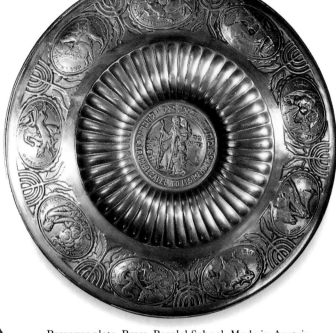

Passover plate. Brass. Bezalel School. Made in Austria in the early 20th century as a prototype. The plate illustrates the song "Chad Gad Ya." *Rabbi Abraham Feldman, Museum of Congregation Beth Israel.*

Detail

Detail

149

Seder Plate. Porcelain. 20th century. Notice the modern adaptation of the traditional patterns. In addition there are six sections for foods. Besides a space for the bitter herbs, an additional one is reserved for horseradish. *National Museum of American Jewish History*. $185.

Seder Plate. Brass and green patina. 1960s Israel. This kind of early Judaica was popular in the years after Israel became a state. It says "Matzah" in the center. *Mrs. Lillian Altman Collection*. $100.

Seder plate. Sterling/bronze. Hana Geber. A limited edition cast from the original. Note that there are only five sections for Passover foods here. *in the spirit gallery*. $975.

Seder plate. Sterling/bronze. Hana Geber. *in the spirit gallery*. $10,000.

Seder Plate/Matzah holder. Alpaca/ brass. Etched vignettes depicting scenes from the Hagaddah. Shelves for the three matzahs. Freiman. Three tiered seder plates have been dated as early as the 18th and 19th centuries. *in the spirit gallery*. $2400.

Seder plate. Hand-painted porcelain. S. Kagan/I. Puski. Like traditional seder plates, this one illustrates the Passover story. This plate shows the parting of the Red Sea and G-d's destruction of the pursuing armies of the Pharaoh. *in the spirit gallery*. $65.

Seder plate. Ceramic. Meira Una. Israeli. *in the spirit gallery*. $2500.

Seder Plate. Recycled aluminum. Judy Pariser. *The National Museum of American Jewish History*. $150.

151

Seder Plate. Hand-blown glass. Kerry Feldman.
Collection of Nancy Berman and Alan Bloch. $500.

Seder plate. Hand-painted porcelain.
I. Puski. *in the spirit gallery.* $65.

Seder Plate. Porcelain. Helena Grosman design.
The National Museum of American Jewish History. $185.

Seder plate. Ceramic. Garson/Pakele.
in the spirit gallery. $450.

Individual seder dishes and the salt water container.

Elijah's Cup. Lenox china. *Robert Bungerz collection* .$75.

Seder Plate. Enamel,glass, copper. Gary Rosenthal. *The National Museum of American Jewish History*. $120.

Elijah's Cup. Ceramic. Garson/Pakele. *The National Museum of American Jewish History*. $185.

Passover dish and candlesticks.
Pharaoh art motif. Art deco. silver.
Many families cherish the traditional
ritual objects passed on by their
families. This silver Passover dish has
the Hebrew word "Karpas" engraved
on the dish. It was used to hold the
green vegetables at the seder. *Albert H.
Bernstein collection.* $1900.

Matzah box. Plexiglass. *Congregation
Keneseth Israel.* $25.

Matzah box. Hand-painted wood. S. Kagan/I. Puski. *in the spirit gallery.* $450.

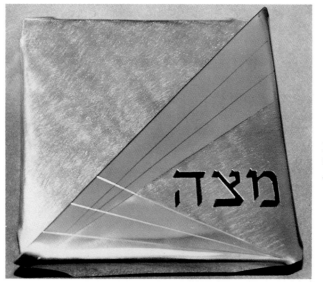

"Matzah is taken." 1992. The Hebrew
letters say "Matzah." Judith E.
Goldstein. USA. *Photography by Judith
E. Goldstein.* $450.

154

Matzah box. Pewter. "Cross to Freedom" Matzah holder. 1992. Judith E. Goldstein. USA. The swirling lines and shapes symbolize the swirling waves of the Red Sea as a backdrop to the three matzahs. *Photography by Judith E. Goldstein.* $800.

Miriam's cup. Glass. Steve Resnick. In the 1990s Jewish feminists wanted to have more of a role in the Passover service and include a reference to Moses's sister Miriam. *The National Museum of American Jewish History.* $185.

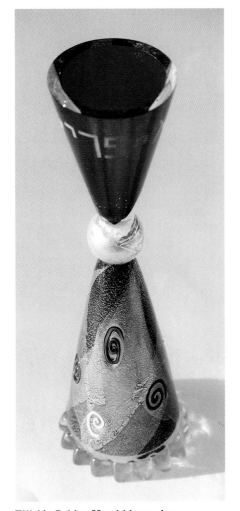

Elijah's Goblet. Hand-blown glass. *Kerry Feldman.*

Miriam's Cup. Pewter/beads of sterling, Swarovski crystal/be Glass. "Sustaining Waters." Judith E. Goldstein. USA. *Photography by Judith E. Goldstein.* $1800.

155

Charoseth dish and spoon. Pewter. "Passover Offerings." 1997. Judith Goldstein. A pyramid design to remind us of the fact that the Jews were slaves in Egypt. The spoon repeats the motif and also shows the swirls symbolizing the parting of the Red Sea. The bowl is unstable to show the precarious balance of freedom. Dish $90. Spoon $40.

Manischewitz Kosher Macaroons. *Wilbur, Sara and Paris Collection.* $100.

Barton's Passover candy tin. 1950s. All leavened foods must cleaned out of the house for Passover and foods specially blessed for Passover are served in their place. Passover candies, cookies and cakes without flour are all part of the Passover holiday celebration. *Wilbur, Sara and Paris collection.* $200.

Barton's Passover candy tin. 1950s. *Wilbur, Sara and Paris collection.* $150.

Pewter wash basin. 1793. This is the bottom part of a wash basin that hung from a wall outside the synagogue. Congregants would wash their hands as part of the Sabbath prayers. *Rabbi Abraham Feldman Museum of the Congregation Beth Israel.*

Washing Laver. Silver. American. 1860. This was given in gratitude "to our distinguished Rabbi and leader Samuel Adler of Temple Emanuel, New York May 25, 1860." *Private collection.*

Above: Wash basin. Horn handles. 19th century. American. *Rabbi Abraham Feldman Museum of the Congregation Beth Israel.*

Left: Washing cup circa 1600s. Copper hand-chased. This copper mug was originally a beer stein. With the addition of a Hebrew blessing it becomes a hand washing basin to be used to wash the hands as proscribed in the Passover seder. *Estate of Gloria Abrams.* $1800.

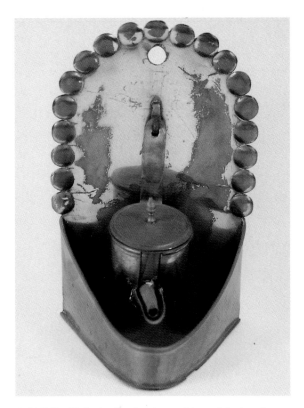

"Al Nitilat Yadayim."....for the washing of the hands. Folk art piece by J. Stuart Green circa 1940. *Brenda Bernstein collection.*

Hand-washing pitcher. Pewter. 1940s-1950s. Often Jews improvised and used secular items for religious purposes. This pitcher was used to wash the hands at seder. *Estate of Norman Yellin.* $75.

Hand-washing basin. Brass. Poland. Late 19th century. *Estate of Max and Jennie Fish.* $300.

Wash cup. Sterling. *in the spirit gallery*. $125.

Wash basin. Pottery. Armenian. *The National Museum of American Jewish History*. $35.

Hand washing pitcher. Hand painted porcelain.
S. Kagan/I. Puski. *in the spirit gallery*. $24.

Chapter 10. Lag B'Omer and Shavuot

Omer counters

Shavuot begins 49 days after Passover and celebrates the day that the Lord gave Moses the Ten Commandments. Shavuot is one of the oldest holidays and one of the three harvest holidays mentioned in the Torah. Today it has become customary for Conservative and Reform congregations to hold a confirmation service during Shavuot. This service announces to the congregation the names of the boys and girls who have completed their Sunday school education.

Lag B'omer, one of the latest Jewish holidays, means the thirty-third day of the counting of the omer and has become a day of joyous celebrations. In Israel it has become customary to have a bonfire. Lag B'Omer also recalls one of the victories of Bar Kochba against the Romans in 135 B.C.E.

Prayer blessing.... "and you excel them all." Hand made paper caste. S. Kagan. USA. *in the spirit gallery*. $1300.

Birkat Habayit.. Blessing over the house. Sterling. *in the spirit gallery*. $110.

The Jewish people have always had a personal relationship with God and have never relied on priests to be their intermediaries or intercede in their behalf. Orthodox Jews observe 613 commandments.

Shecheyanu Plate. Hand-painted porcelain. S.Kagan/*I. Puski.*
"Shecheyanu, vihigeyanu, lazman hazeh....Blessed art thou, O Lord
our God, king of the universe, who has kept us alive and given us
strength and made it possible for us to reach this happy day." *in the
spirit gallery.* $275.

Omer counter. 19th century. Wood. Made out of an old cigar box.
The National Museum of American Jewish History.

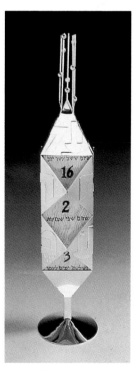

Omer Calendar. Silver, fabricated and applique
parchment, printed and embossed. Moshe
Zabari (b. 1935). 1993. *Courtesy of Alan and Pat
Davidson, New York. Photography by D. R.
Guthrie, Jerusalem.*

Omer Counter. Hand-painted wood. Shirley Kagan USA 1987. The omer calendar
records each of the 49 days between Passover and Shavuot. *Rabbi Abraham Feldman
Museum of the Congregation Beth Israel.* $200.

Chapter 11. Weddings, Bar and Bat Mitzvah, Birth and Circumcision

Ketubot, wedding goblets, wedding rings, wimpels, kipahs

Rituals accompany every aspect of Jewish life from birth to death. Jewish couples are married under a chuppah and sign a Ketubah, a written document, signed in front of the rabbi and witnesses, showing a commitment to the marriage vows. It guarantees that both the man and women will honor the wedding vows. Although originally considered a marriage contract, today most young couples regard it as more symbolic.

Since a ketubah was originally considered to be a legally binding document, traditional ketubot were written by trained calligraphers. The earliest known ketubot date from the 11th and 12th centuries. Early Italian ketubot are among the most ornate and beautiful.

During the marriage service, the bridal couple drinks from a double marriage cup and after the ceremony, the groom smashes a glass goblet under his foot. Today many couples save the glass shards as a symbol of their union.

There are two explanations for the breaking of the glass. One is that since the marriage ceremony is one of life's greatest joys, one should not forget Judaism's great sorrow that the Temple has been destroyed and never rebuilt.

Another explanations refers to the superstitions of the Middle Ages and the fear of the constant presence of evil spirits and the evil eye. It was believed that loud noises frightened evil spirits.

Circumcision is the ceremony held eight days after the birth of a male child. It is said that when Abraham agreed to sacrifice his first born son Isaac to God, he showed his devotion to God. Since then it has been said that the circumcision ceremony, the cutting away of the foreskin of the penis of a baby boy, continues this covenant between God and the Hebrew people.

Circumcision is performed by a mohel, a rabbi who has been specially trained to perform this act. Usually the mohel uses a special knife and puts the baby on a chair called Elijah's chair.

In 16th century Germany, it became the custom to take the wimpel, or swaddling clothes that were wrapped around a boy during his circumcision, and make torah binders out of them and embroider his name, his birth date, and the blessing that he grow up to study Torah, marry under the chuppah and lead a life of tzedakah.

Folk art painting. *Edythe Siegel Gallery of American-Jewish Folk Art.*

Chuppah sculpture. Silver/bronze. Hana Geber. *in the spirit gallery*. $3400.

Marriage ring. 19th-20th century. Italian. *Rabbi Abraham Feldman Museum of the Congregation Beth Israel.*

Wedding Plate. Silver. Bier. Israel. *in the spirit gallery*.

Wedding goblet. Ceramic. *Private collection.*

Ketubah case. Hand-painted wood/parchment. S. Kagan/I. Puski. *in the spirit gallery.* $2400.

Wedding Frame. "Shaddai...G-d is always before me. Hand-painted wood. *in the spirit gallery.* $95.

Wedding box. Hand painted wood. S.Kagan/I. Puski. *in the spirit gallery.* $395.

Wedding Cup. "May G-d be as happy with you as the bridegroom is with his bride." *in the spirit gallery.* $185.

Wedding Cups. Hand-painted porcelain. S. Kagan/I.Puski. *in the spirit gallery.* $185.

Matriarch cup. Glass and brass sculpture. Linda Casein. *The National Museum of American Jewish History.* $150.

Above: "Who is strong above all else. Who is blessed above all else. Who is great above all else. He who blesses, bless the bridegroom and bride." *The National Museum of American Jewish History.*

Right: Cohen wedding goblet. *The National Museum of American Jewish History.* $285.

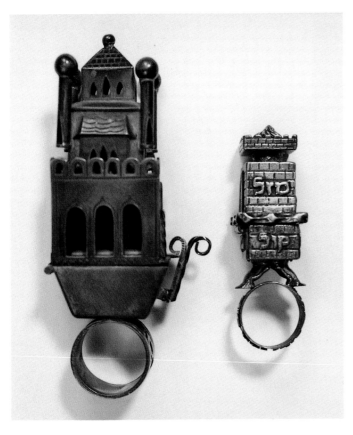

Wedding rings. silver. Antique circa 1900. *in the spirit gallery*. $1800. Reproduction $110.

When Rabbi Abraham Feldman married members of his Confirmation classes he insisted that they wear this service star to show that they had been confirmed.

It is traditional for Jewish brides and grooms to sign a marriage contract called a Ketubah. The marriage is held under a canopy called a Chuppah. After the ceremony often the Ketubah is hung on the walls of the new home. Sometimes the bridal couple will drink from a double marriage cup, in which two cups form one.

Caucasian silver gilt marriage belt. Late 19th century. *Rabbi Abraham Feldman Museum of the Congregation Beth Israel.*

The following ketubah blanks come from *The National Museum of American Jewish History*. $200-300.

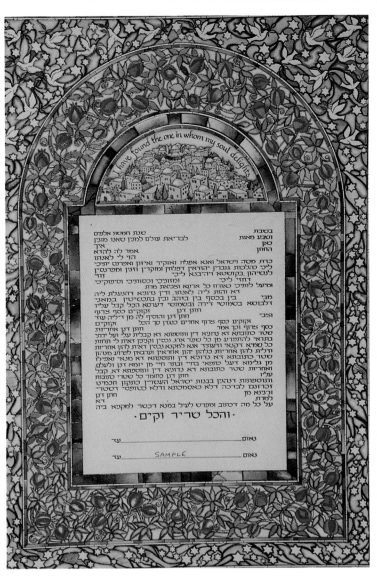

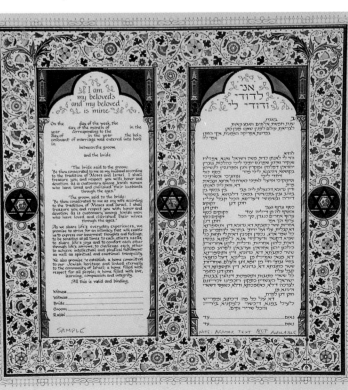

167

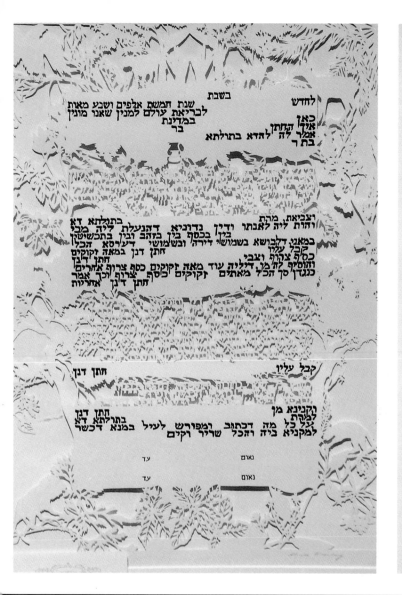

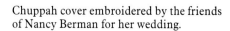

Chuppah cover embroidered by the friends of Nancy Berman for her wedding.

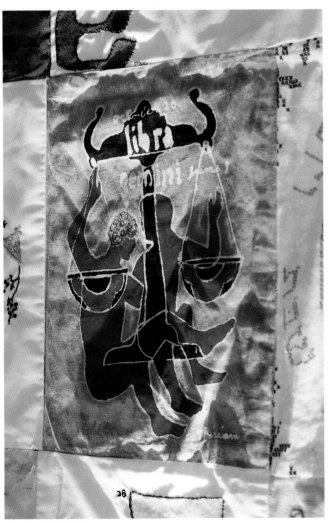

A 19th century circumcision scene. *Wilbur, Sara, and Paris Pierce Collection.*

Chapter 12. Yahrzeit Candles

Jewish people are diligent in keeping alive the memory of the dead, and every year on the anniversary of the death of a loved one, a yahrzeit candle is lit and burns for twenty-four hours. Yahrzeit lights are usually short, squat candles. Special electric lights can also be used.

Yarhzeits are also observed during the High Holidays when the names of the dead are recalled during the service. Many Jews visit the cemeteries on the Sunday between Rosh Hashonah and Yom Kippur.

A three dimensional card showing the Jewish cemetery in Prague. Sadly the Jewish people have been persecuted for their religion for over 2000 years and death and annihilation have been a constant part of their history. The Jewish Cemetery in Prague is one of the most mystical and romantic sites. Grave stones stand at precarious angles, crowding one another in a baroque maze. The scene is at once bizarre, macabre and tragic.

Yahrzeit light. 20th century. *Private collection.*

Yahrzeit candle. Plexiglass. wood. Brenda Bernstein design. *in the spirit gallery.*

Yahrzeit candle holder. *Congregation Keneseth Israel.* $35.

Yahrzeit memorial sculpture. circa 1919. White metal. Cerilian writing on the back. *Albert H. Bernstein collection.* $2200.

Yahrzeit candle. "May their souls be bound in everlasting life." Cobalt. Rothschild. *in the spirit gallery.* $85.

Yahrzeit candle holder. *Congregation Keneseth Israel.* $35.

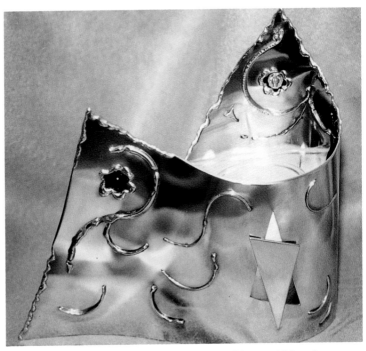

The Yahrzeit light is a memorial light lit every year on the anniversary of the death of a loved one.

Yahrzeit lamp, pewter, with beads of black onyx and Swarovski Austrian crystal with an Aurora Borealis finish. Judith E. Goldstein. 1991. USA. "Let Their Memory Be a Blessing Forever." Says the artist, "this yahrzeit sculpture wraps around the traditional yahrzeit candle just as our memories of a lost one wrap around us to envelop and sustain. The open form of the Star of David allows constant viewing of the flame itself; and invites us to meditate on our memories stimulated by the changing glow of the flame thrown upon the background representing Paradise. *Photography by Judith E. Goldstein.* $500.

Chapter 13. Kasruth: Keeping Kosher
Kosher plates and kosher foods

Keeping kosher is one of the commandments given to the Jews in the Bible. It is commanded not to mix milk or dairy foods and meat. Kosher butchers are trained in the laws of kashruth and slaughter animals in a special way. For hundreds of years observant Jews would not eat in public places for fear that the table would not be kosher. Until the 1980s, ocean liners maintained a separate kosher kitchen and china and silverware were stamped with the kosher seal.

Kosher Stamp. American. circa 1920s. Jews who keep Kosher have kosher china for milk and meat. The Laws of Kasruth command the Jews not to mix milk and meat and to not eat animals with a cloven hoof. *Private collection.*

Above: Kosher butcher knife and painted wooden case. 20th century American. *The National Museum of American Jewish History.*

Right: Kosher fish knives used on board Cunard ships. Until the 1980s, many ocean liners had separate kosher kitchens. *Private collection.*

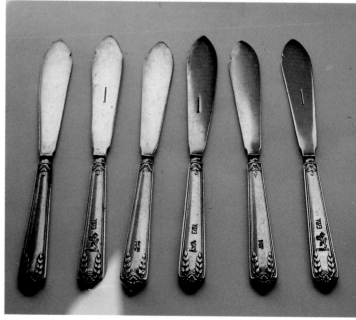

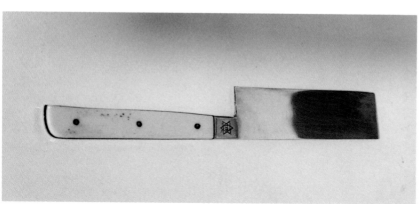

Shohet knife. 19th century. *Private collection.*

Milk and meat china used on board the ocean liner Queen Mary. English bone china. Until the 1980s, many ocean liners and cruise ships maintained a separate kosher kitchen and used separate china for milk and meat. $130.

A kosher demi-tasse cup and saucer from the Queen Mary, served with meat. *Collection of Alexander Goldfarb.* $300.

Octagon dish washing powder. *Wilbur, Sara, and Paris Pierce Collection.* $200.

Detail

173

Kosher soaps

Kosher ginger.

Kosher spices

Spices. *Collection of Wilbur, Sara and Paris Pierce.* $100 each.

Tin can

Light bulb

Gold Star tool bits.

Chapter 14. Secular Judaica: The American Experience

The first Jewish immigration to America began in 1654, when twenty-three Jews, fearing that Portuguese occupation of Brazil, heralded a return to the practices of the Inquisition, fled their homes in Recife, Brazil, and sailed north, seeking religious freedom in the colony of New Amsterdam in what is now New York City.

The next year, 1655, the first Torah arrived in America from Amsterdam, and the Jews were able to hold services and publicly follow their religious precepts. And within a few years, despite some opposition from the local Dutch governors, they established what would become the first important Jewish community in America. Soon there were four more Jewish communities in Savannah(1733), Newport (1750), Charleston, (1750) and Philadelphia (1760). By 1763 the Jews of Newport dedicated the Touro Synagogue which remains today the oldest surviving synagogue structure in North America. The first Jewish prayer book for the High Holy Days was published in New York in 1791 and kosher food was served following the ratification of the Constitution of Pennsylvania. Soon Jews were mingling in both Jewish and non-Jewish societies. Among the best known were the Philadelphians Haym Solomon, a friend of George Washington, and the Gratz family, one of the most cultured families in colonial Philadelphia.

With the emancipation of the Jews by Napoleon in France in the 19th century, Jews began to make more and more of secular presence and their names became known outside of the Jewish communities.

By the 1840s more and more Jews were heading to the American West, establishing Jewish communities at Santa Fe and in Colorado and California. Soon thousands of German Jewish immigrants came to America and added to the American Jewish experience.

With the mass immigrations of the late 19th and early twentieth centuries, Jews poured into the lower East Side of New York and soon made an impact on the cultural life of the city. Jews were vital to the growth of the vaudeville theater, the movie industry, the entertainment world and even the world of sports. One of the first Jewish major league baseball players was Lyman Pike. One of the best known in the 1920s and 1930s was Moe Berg. Years later there was Hank Greenberg.

In the 1950s, my Sunday School teachers talked of Israel as a mysterious, exotic land where Jews worshiped freely as Jews and everything was Jewish. We were told that a visit to Israel would be like a walk through Biblical history. My ideas of Jewish heroes were formed by movie heroes such as Charleton Heston's Moses and Paul Newman's role in "Exodus." Today there are Jewish comic book super heroes like "Shaloman."

In the 1960s and 1970s my views of Israel were formed by the first hand reports of a land transformed by sabras, tough skinned men and women who pioneered the founding of modern Israel and created an escape hatch for the future to insure that never again would another Hitler threaten Jews with extinction. I was enthralled by the stories of American women, who as ardent Zionists, had traveled to Palestine in the 1920s and 1930s and found not a land of milk and honey, but a land of thorns, desert and hardship.

Until the 1970s, Israel had been a mystical dream. For years, I had sat at our family Passover table and said the words, "Next year in Jerusalem." In 1970 I made it, and along with hundreds of other Jews, I burst into tears as the sounds of Hatikvah, the Israeli national anthem filled the cabin of the El Al plane. I was the first member of my family to visit the promised land, and when I made my first visit to the Western Wall, I stuffed prayers in its cracks for all the members of my family.

By the 1980s Levy's Bread had introduced the popular campaign, "You Don't Have to be Jewish to Like Levy's Bread," and suddenly it seemed as if everyone was Jewish and everyone wanted to share in the Jewish experience. In fact, the 1980s symbolized a new era for Jewish culture. Not only bagels, but Jewish foods, Jewish comedians, Jewish writers, and Yiddish words became part of the mainstream culture.

A first time visit to Israel is often just as surprising to Jews as it is to non-Jews. Jews arrive expecting to find an intact Eastern European Jewish world, a feast of "bagels and delis." Non-Jews expect to see the holy land of their bible, unchanged. Both are in for a surprise. The Israel of the 1990s is more complex.

The Israel of the present is first and foremost a Middle Eastern country that has been emerging rapidly into the twentieth century, and what remains unique about the country Israel is its Jewishness. On first glance, the most visible examples of Judaism are the ubiquitous presence of Jewish symbols such as the Star of David, the widespread use the Hebrew language, and the observance of the Sabbath. Buildings, stores, restaurant menus, newspapers, buses, road signs, movies, are all in Hebrew. And on most city streets is the exotic presence of the Orthodox Jews who are still wearing the traditional clothes prescribed by their rabbis years ago in Eastern Europe- long black robes, black shoes, long starched white shorts, tall fur hats, side curls dangling along the sides of their faces, the fringes of their prayer shawls hanging out from under their shirts.

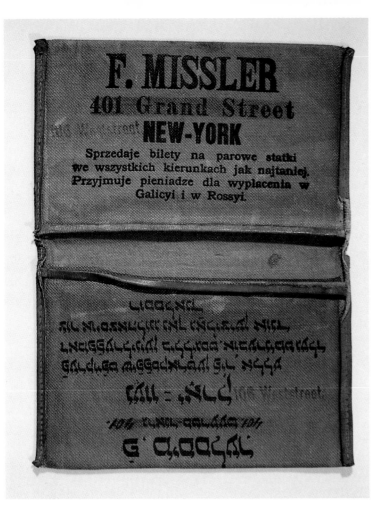

Ship ticket container. Passage to the New World of America marked the renaissance of the Jewish people. America while not a country with streets paved with gold, did provide the Jewish people with incredible opportunities for growth both personally, spiritually and economically. *Wilbur, Sara, and Paris Pierce Collection.* $100.

Symbolic certificates for 129 round trips in the passage of life were popular among late 19th century and early 20th century Jews and were given out at synagogues. *Wilbur, Sara, and Paris Pierce Collection.*

"Hativah" became the national anthem of Israel. *Wilbur, Sara, and Paris Pierce Collection.* $45.

Jews made their mark in the entertainment world especially in the Yiddish Theater and in Vaudeville. *Wilbur, Sara, and Paris Pierce Collection.* $45.

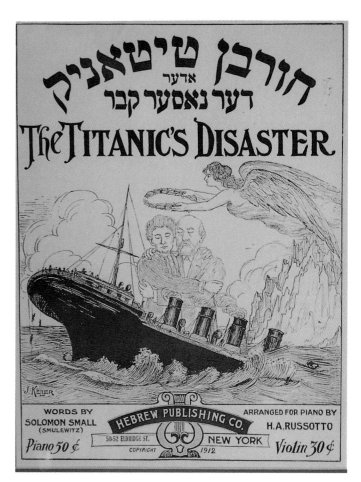

Al Jolson was one of the greatest entertainers of his day. *Wilbur, Sara, and Paris Pierce Collection.* $95.

The Titanic disaster reached into the Jewish community and the example of Isidor and Ida Strauss was an inspiration for popular Yiddish songs and stories. *Private collection.* $225.

Above: Eddie Cantor was another show business Jewish great. *Wilbur, Sara, and Paris Pierce Collection.* $65.

Right: Another Al Jolson album. *Wilbur, Sara, and Paris Pierce Collection.* $95.

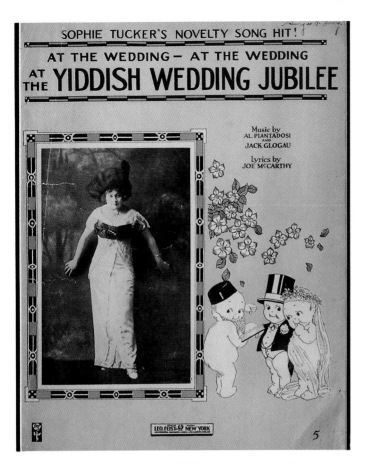

Sophie Tucker was another. *Wilbur, Sara, and Paris Pierce Collection.* $65.

Jerry Her... ...and Honey" was an instant hit in 1961. It starred
Robert Wee... ...nzell and Molly Picon who was best known for
her roles in the... ...heater. *Courtesy of Jacqueline Baker.*

Magazine photo, *Sunday News*, December 10, 1962. "After 50 years in the theatre, Molly Picon romps in her first Broadway musical. She's shown here at the climax of the 'Independence Day Hora,' an exciting dance that lifts audiences' spirits as high as Molly." *Courtesy of Jacqueline Baker.*

103 MORRIS BERG
Catcher Boston Red Sox

Born: New York City   March 2, 1903
Bats: Right   Throws: Right
Height: 6' 1"   Weight: 185 lbs.

Moe Berg is regarded as the most educated man in baseball, having graduated from Princeton, Columbia, and the Sorbonne, France. Berg has been a major-league ball player for 18 years, starting in 1923. He is known as one of the smartest catchers in the game, because of his ability to handle young pitchers. He started with Brooklyn as a shortstop, later shifting to catcher, and has seen action with the Chicago White Sox, Cleveland Indians, and Washington Senators, as well as the Red Sox. Moe spends his off-seasons practicing law, and globe-trotting, having been around the world several times. He also speaks fluently eight different languages.

PLAY BALL—America

This is one of a series of 250 pictures of leading baseball players. Save to get them all.
GUM, INC., Philadelphia, Pa. Printed in U. S. A.

Jews became famous in the world of sports. Morris "Moe" Berg was one of the greatest players of his day. *Paris Pierce collection*. $500.

Detail

—No. 158—
MORRIS (MOE) BERG
WASHINGTON SENATORS

Became a catcher by accident. Was an infielder with the Chicago White Sox in 1927 when injuries to the catching staff caused manager Ray Schalk to look around for assistance. Berg stepped in and filled the bill. He has been working behind the bat ever since.

He is a graduate of Princeton and has also studied law at Columbia University.

Born in New York City, March 2, 1902.

White Sox bought Berg from Reading Club in 1926. Joined Washington last year.

6 feet, 170 lbs. Bats right handed. Last year batted .236 in 75 games.

This is one of a series of 240 Baseball Stars

BIG LEAGUE
CHEWING GUM

GOUDEY GUM CO.   BOSTON

Made by the originators of
INDIAN GUM

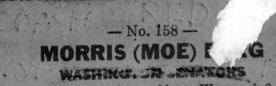

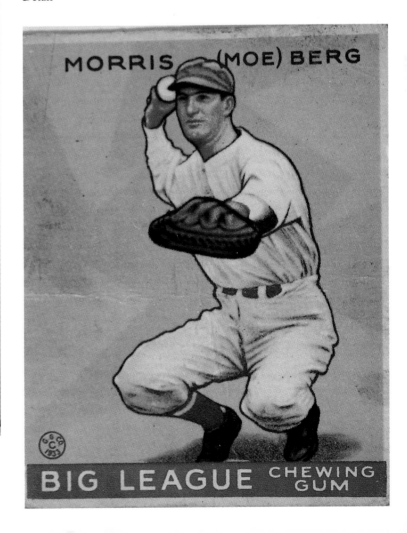

Above: Moe Berg. *Paris Pierce collection*. $500.

Right: Front view of the card.

Shaloman is a new-style Jewish hero. $2.

Poster for US War Bonds. World War I. *Wilbur, Sara, and Paris Pierce Collection.* $1200.

Ballot box. 1854. Ladies Deborah Society of Temple Beth Israel. *Rabbi Abraham Feldman Museum of the Congregation Beth Israel.*

1918 War Relief poster *"Food for Peace."* This poster was printed in three languages: English, Yiddish, and Italian. $1500.

Brass hinged box, "Moe Levy, 1897, Clothing, N.Y."

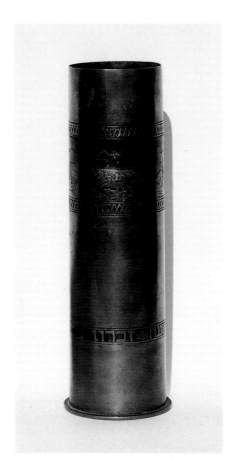

Left: Shell art. 1917. This was made from a brass shell casing from World War I artillery. *Private collection.*

Above: Detail

Trade items. Jewish merchants, like their non-Jewish counterparts, realized the importance of public relations. *Private collection.* $100.

Trade cards, trade buttons. *Private collection.* $150.

An early 20th-century confirmation notebook. *Rabbi Abraham Feldman Museum of the Congregation Beth Israel.* $25.

1900s sampler. American. *Private collection.*

Early 20th-century confirmation class portrait. *Rabbi Abraham Feldman Museum of the Congregation Beth Israel.* $25.

Late 19th-century certificate for good teaching. *Private collection.*

Early 1893-1897 gold watches manufactured in Illinois. *Private collection.*

Ashtray in the shape of an old oil lamp. Pal-Bel green metal. 1950s. *Private collection.*

Sisterhood cookbooks. 1940s-1950s. *The National Museum of American Jewish History.* $35.

Olivewood picture of the Western Wall. Early 20th century. Prior to the Six Day War, the western wall of Solomon's Temple was called the Wailing Wall as a derogatory term; after the Six Day War it was once again called the Western Wall. *Private collection.*

Book ends. Green patina metals. Pal Bel. 1950s. Israel. *Private collection.*

Three baseball caps the Phillies, the Mets and the Yankees in Hebrew script. *The National Museum of American Jewish History.* $24.

Olivewood camel souvenir. 1950s. *Private collection.*

"You Don't Have to be Jewish to like Levy's" is one of the most popular advertising slogans of the 1980s. $800.

The walls of Jerusalem.

Chicken Soup the universal Jewish remedy for all ills. *Wilbur, Sara, and Paris Pierce Collection.*

Shalom and peace. "City of Peace." Bruce David. *Edythe Siegel Gallery of American-Jewish Folk Art.*

The hills beyond Jerusalem.

The Lions' Gate or St. Stephen's Gate. Note the pairs of lions on either side of the entrance way. This is the northeastern entrance to the Temple esplanade. Beyond the gate is the Via Dolorosa of the Christians.

The Western Wall of the Temple has become a religious site for the Jews. Pilgrims come from all over the world and squeeze crumpled prayers into its cracks.

Chapter 15. Modern Judaism

The Jewish people have always felt a personal relationship with God and have never relied on priests to be their sole intermediaries or intercede in their behalf. Orthodox Jews observe more than 613 different commandments in their daily lives.

In the years following the birth of the state of Israel, Jewish artists not only began to explore new materials and new designs for traditional objects of observance, but twentieth century Jews have added new religious customs.

One of the biggest areas of change has been in regard to a more active female role in Judaism. Many women have felt left out of Jewish rituals, and have redefined their roles as Jewish women.

Twenty years ago, when my aunt Lillian called to announce that she was going to be Bat Mitzvahed at the age of 65, I was surprised. Bar Mitzvahs had traditionally been a male only ceremony celebrating the coming of age for thirteen year old Jewish boys. It wasn't until the 1960s and 1970s that Bat Mitzvah, the female equivalent, became popular among young Jewish girls.

My aunt was more than thirty years older than the other women in her class. It was unusual for an adult Jewish woman to take an active part in her religion outside the home. Most of her contemporaries maintained the traditional Jewish female role of lighting the Friday night candles at home, preparing the holiday meals and encouraging their children to attend services and Sunday schools.

Today not only are more Jewish women choosing to become Bat Mitzvah, but more and more are taking an active role in Jewish observances. There are women rabbis and women cantors and as these women have become increasingly involved they have begun to feminize the rituals and religious objects and take a deeper look into the Torah for their Jewish female heritage.

Beginning in the 1980s Jewish feminists have held Feminist Passover Seders and introduced the custom of drinking from a Miriam's cup to honor Moses's sister. And during the High Holiday services it is no longer the exception to see women being called to the bema to read from the Torah.

A Final Word

Writing this book has been an exciting quest. It has been astounding to see the emergence of so many outstanding Jewish artists so passionate about creating Judaica. These artists have recognized that Jews want beautiful objects with which to celebrate their religion. The result has been an explosion of creativity, imagination, and innovation that has infused the rituals of a 5000-year-old religion with objects that reflect twentieth-century modernism.

Whether an object is silver, gleaming stainless steel, funky ceramic, or plastic, the commandment is the same, "Thou shalt love the Lord thy God with all thy heart and with all thy soul."

Bibliography

Berman, Nancy, *The Art of Hanukkah*, Hugh Lauter Levin Associates, Inc., 1996.

Berman, Nancy, *Moshe Zabari: A Twenty-five Year Retrospective*, The Jewish Museum of New York, 1986.

Diamant, Anita and Howard Cooper, *Living a Jewish Life*, Harper Collins, New York, 1991.

Epstein, Morris, *All About Jewish Holidays and Customs*, Ktav Publishing House, New York, 1959.

Greenberg, Betty and Althea Silverman, *The Jewish Home Beautiful*, The Women's League of the United Synagogue, 1947.

"New Beginnings" the Skirball Museum Collections and Inaugural Exhibition, Skirball Cultural Center, Los Angeles, 1996.

Ouaknin, Marc-Alain, *Symbols of Judaism*, Editions Assouline, Paris, 1995.

Purdy, Susan Gold, *Jewish Holidays*. Lippincott Company, Philadelphia and New York, 1969.

Resources

Judaica Shops

Judaica shops exist everywhere; today most synagogues and temples have their own shops. We thank the following for all their help:

in the spirit Gallery
460 E. 79th Street
New York City, New York 10021
212-861-5222

The National Museum of American Jewish History
Independence Mall East, 55 North 5th Street
Philadelphia, PA.19106-2197
215-923-5978

Audrey's
The Skirball Cultural Center and Museum
2701 N. Sepulveda Blvd.
Los Angeles, California 90049
310-440-4611

Congregation Keneseth Israel
2227 West Chew Street
Allentown, PA 18104-5592
610-435-9074

Rabbi Abraham Feldman Museum of Congregation Temple Beth Israel
701 Farmington Avenue
West Hartford, Connecticut 06105
860-233-8245

Judith E. Goldstein
66 Windshire Dr.
South Windsor, Connecticut 06074

Edythe Siegel Gallery of American-Jewish Folk Art
2362 High Ridge Road
Stamford, Connecticut 06903
203-322-6131

Wilbur Pierce
1627 Walnut Street
Philadelphia, PA 19103

Kerry Jay Feldman
P.O. Box 4318
Breckenridge, Colorado 80424

Index Of Artist Names